JOHN LENNON
ALL I WANT IS THE TRUTH

JOHN

ALL I WANT IS

VIKING

a photographic biography by

Elizabeth Partridge

LENNON

THE TRUTH

VIKING

Published by Penguin Group

Penguin Young Readers Group, 345 Hudson Street, New York, New York 10014, U.S.A.

Penguin Group (Canada), 90 Eglinton Avenue East, Suite 700, Toronto, Ontario, Canada M4P 2Y3

(a division of Pearson Penguin Canada Inc.)

Penguin Books Ltd, 80 Strand, London WC2R 0RL, England

Penguin Ireland, 25 St Stephen's Green, Dublin 2, Ireland

(a division of Penguin Books Ltd)

Penguin Group (Australia), 250 Camberwell Road, Camberwell, Victoria 3124, Australia

(a division of Pearson Australia Group Pty Ltd)

Penguin Books India Pvt Ltd, 11 Community Centre, Panchsheel Park, New Delhi – 110 017, India

Penguin Group (NZ), Cnr Airborne and Rosedale Roads, Albany, Auckland 1310, New Zealand

(a division of Pearson New Zealand Ltd)

Penguin Books (South Africa) (Pty) Ltd, 24 Sturdee Avenue, Rosebank, Johannesburg 2196, South Africa

Penguin Books Ltd, Registered Offices: 80 Strand, London WC2R 0RL, England

First published in 2005 by Viking, a division of Penguin Young Readers Group

10 9 8 7 6 5 4 3 2 1

LIBRARY OF CONGRESS CATALOGING-IN-PUBLICATION DATA

Partridge, Elizabeth.

John Lennon : all I want is the truth : a biography / by Elizabeth Partridge.

p. cm.

Includes bibliographical references and index.

ISBN 0-670-05954-4 (hardcover)

1. Lennon, John, 1940–1980—Juvenile literature. 2. Rock musicians—England—Biography—Juvenile literature.
I. Title.   ML3930.L34P37 2005   782.42166'092—dc22   2005011850

Manufactured in China   Set in Perpetua and Bagheera   Book design by Jim Hoover

To Jill Davis

CONTENTS

INTRODUCTION
GIVE PEACE A CHANCE
1969

"In me secret heart I wanted to write something that would take over 'We Shall Overcome.' . . . I thought, 'Why isn't somebody writing one for the people now?'"

ON THE MORNING of March 25, 1969, more than fifty reporters jammed the corridor outside Room 902 of the Amsterdam Hilton. Inside were newly married John Lennon and Yoko Ono. They'd announced that a "happening" would take place in their bed during their honeymoon. The press was invited.

"These guys were sweating to fight to get in first because they thought we were going to be making love in bed," John said. He figured it was because the cover of their recent album, *Two Virgins*, featured a photo of them standing nude in front of their unmade bed. "Because we'd been naked," he explained. "Naked, bed, John and Yoko, sex."

When the door opened and the reporters shoved in, they found John and Yoko sitting side by side in bed, dressed in white. John wore pajamas, Yoko a demure nightgown with long sleeves and a high neck. They said they would stay in bed for a week to "protest against all the suffering and violence in the world."

There was plenty to protest against. The civil rights movement, begun so optimistically with marchers linking arms and singing "We Shall Overcome," had been shattered by the assassination of Martin Luther King, Jr. Race riots ricocheted through the streets of New York, Los Angeles, London, and Johannesburg. As the Vietnam War reached new levels of ferocity, protestors poured into the streets. Cops hurled tear gas canisters and waded into the crowds, cracking skulls with their billy clubs. Catholics rioted in Londonderry; Soviet tanks rumbled through Prague chasing down unarmed students. The issues were radically different, but the frustration, alienation, and profound distrust of authority were worldwide.

Against the staggering violence, the "bed-in" seemed naive, even nonsensical. Many cynically regarded it as self-indulgent, dubbing them "Joko." A radio interviewer asked John how it felt to have people jeering at him. "It's part of our policy not to be taken seriously," John replied defensively. "And we stand a better chance under that guise, because all the serious people like Martin Luther King and Kennedy and Gandhi got shot."

John was tired of appearing apolitical, tired of being muzzled as a Beatle, constantly told to keep his political views to himself so he wouldn't negatively affect the group's popularity. After six years in the international spotlight as a pop star, he was acutely savvy about the media. It was time to use the attention for something important.

In May, John and Yoko held a "Bed-in for Peace" in Montreal. The close proximity to the United States allowed them to do hundreds of radio, TV, and newspaper interviews with the American press.

John was intense, urgent, and passionate. He wasn't under any illusion he could change the policies of world leaders, just because he and Yoko said, "Peace, brother." He was twenty-eight years old, Yoko thirty-five. Activists had recently popularized the slogan, "Never trust anyone over thirty!" Forget heads of state, presidents, and prime ministers. John knew who he was after: "Youth is the future," he said. "If we can get inside their minds and tell them to think in favour of non-violence, we'll be satisfied."

John and Yoko fervently condemned America's aggression in Vietnam: The United States had now dropped more bombs on Vietnam than all the bombs dropped in World War II on Europe and Asia combined.

"All I'm saying is peace," John explained repeatedly. "Give it a *chance*." Sitting in bed with Yoko, surrounded by enormous bouquets of white carnations, repeating his message over and over again, John quickly and effortlessly formed his peace message into song lyrics. He posted

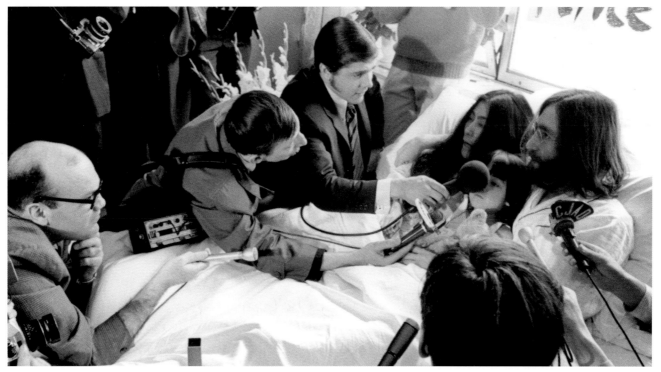

John and Yoko speak to the press in May 1969 at the Queen Elizabeth Hotel in Montreal during their weeklong "Bed-in for Peace." Yoko's daughter Kyoko lies in between them.

the words on the wall and taught the song to his eclectic, enthusiastic group of visitors.

"Give Peace a Chance" was released just weeks later on July 4, 1969. The tune was catchy, deceptively simple. John's voice was energized, full of conviction, the lyrics typical of his brilliant wordplay—funny, with a sharp, biting edge. The song hit the Top Forty on the pop charts in England and America, then flew out into the streets, a synergetic connection between people and the right song at the right time. It wasn't hyped, it wasn't promoted. The song just took hold.

On November 15, 1969, two hundred and fifty thousand people gathered in Washington, D.C., to protest the Vietnam War. In England, the demonstration was broadcast on television. John watched as the enormous gathering of people, stretching as far as the eye could see, sang his song. He was amazed. They seemed to sing "forever, and not stopping," he said. "It was one of the biggest moments of my life."

In the months and years to come, his song would fill the air at rallies, marches, and candle-lit vigils around the world. In a flash of inspiration, John had written an anthem for the peace movement.

1

MENDIPS

1940-1952

"It's that same problem I had when I was five: 'There is something wrong with me because I seem to see things other people don't see. Am I crazy, or am I a genius?'"

JOHN LENNON WAS different, and he knew it. It wasn't that he was being raised by his aunt and uncle while his mother, never divorced from his father, lived nearby with another man and their children. It was something inside him, something in the way he viewed the world. No one else seemed to understand: not his teachers, his aunt and uncle, his friends. It made him angry, tough, and afraid.

On the night of October 9, 1940, German war planes arced gracefully over the swelling Irish Sea, took their bearings from the bright glow of neutral Dublin, and swung east. Engines purring, they headed straight for the English port town of Liverpool. English air-raid sirens howled as bombs hit with deafening explosions, tearing massive holes in the streets, smashing buildings, blowing people to bits.

During a lull in the shelling, Mimi Stanley Smith ran alone through the blacked-out streets of Liverpool to the Oxford Street Maternity Hospital. Her sister Julia had just given birth, and nothing was going to stop Mimi from seeing the baby.

John stands in the doorway at Mendips, the house where he lived with his aunt Mimi and uncle George in Woolton, a village on the edge of Liverpool.

Damage from German bombing of Liverpool the night John was born, October 9, 1940. Every morning after a German air raid, Liverpool officials went out with cameras to document the destruction.

At the hospital Mimi sat next to her sister's bed, admiring Julia's newborn son, demanding the nurses find a softer blanket to swaddle him in. Julia, in a small, defiant show of courage and patriotism, named her son John Winston Lennon, honoring the irascible Winston Churchill, the English prime minister who held their safety and future in his hands.

Suddenly the warning sirens began wailing again. More German bombers were on their way. The nurses thrust John under Julia's sturdy bed and urged Mimi to go down to the cellar, but she refused. Instead, she headed back to the streets. Patrolling wardens shouted at her to get under shelter. "Oh, be quiet," she said, dodging in and out of doorways as she ran the two miles back home. She told her parents, "It's a boy and he's beautiful, he's the best one of all." Her father looked up at her and said, "Oh heck, he *would* be."

No one in Julia's family approved of Alfred Lennon, Julia's husband. Raised in the Bluecoat Orphanage in Liverpool, he'd left at fifteen and found work as a ship's waiter. When Freddie docked in Liverpool, he and Julia went to the cinema or out to the pubs. Sometimes Freddie would serenade Julia at her parents' house, and she'd play her banjo and ukulele for him. Freddie's work on ships, his lower-class Liverpool accent, known as a "Scouser" accent, and his lack of money all put him beneath the Stanley family.

Julia was twenty-four when she and Freddie impulsively married in December 1938. "I'll never forget that day," Mimi said. "Julia came home, threw a piece of paper on the table and said, 'There, that's it. I've married him.'"

Early in 1940, shortly after Freddie managed a Christmas visit, Julia discovered she was pregnant. It was a difficult, nerve-wracking time. In September 1939, England had thrown its weight against Hitler and entered World War II. Food was rationed, bomb shelters hastily set up, gas masks issued to civilians. Just weeks before Julia gave birth, the Germans launched an all-out bombardment of Liverpool that lasted through October.

People were living in "bug-ridden, lice-ridden, rat-ridden, lousy hellholes," Bessie Braddock (middle of crowd, in black), a member of the House of Commons, declared. Though John lived in a good neighborhood, many of Liverpool's poor lived in crowded, substandard housing. The problem was worsened by German bombing.

Tens of thousands of children, mothers, and infants were evacuated, but Julia and John remained in Liverpool with Julia's parents on Newcastle Road in the Penny Lane district. At an early age, John showed precocious signs of sharing his mother's determined, impetuous nature. From his high chair he grabbed for the spoon, eager to feed himself, and before he was a year old he was up on his feet, cruising around the house. Julia, never much for responsibility, managed with the help of her four sisters and a portion of Freddie's ship's wages.

The money stopped abruptly when John was about eighteen months old. Freddie had been thrown in jail, caught with liquor stolen from the ship's cargo. Knowing that Julia enjoyed a good time, Freddie sent her a letter from jail encouraging her to go out and enjoy herself.

Julia didn't need to be told twice. American GIs had poured into Britain, bringing cigarettes, silk stockings, jazzy American records. Julia headed for the dances being held in clubs and halls and jitterbugged the nights away. John's cousin Stanley, seven years older, was delighted by the American GIs marching up and down the streets and careening around in their jeeps. With sweets nearly impossible to get because of rationing, Stanley and John would run outside and beg treats from the GIs whenever they saw them. "Got any gum, chum?" they'd ask.

In the fall of 1944, Freddie made a visit to Liverpool for the first time in eighteen months. Julia had shocking news for him: She was pregnant by another man. Though Freddie said he'd accept the child as his own, Julia was afraid he'd throw her unfaithfulness back in her face later. Julia's scandalized father had the last word: The child would be put up for adoption, or he'd throw Julia and John out of the house.

In May 1945, Germany was forced to surrender. But the mood at the Stanley's house was not all celebratory. A few weeks later, on June 19, Julia gave birth to a girl she named Victoria Elizabeth. Adopted by Margaret and Peder Pedersen, the baby was renamed Ingrid, and Julia never saw her again.

Soon after giving up the baby, Julia met a new man, Bobby Dykins. A tall, handsome waiter at the stately Adelphi Hotel, Bobby loved ballroom dancing and took Julia out to tango and rumba. Julia's family was scandalized all over again. Julia didn't care. She moved into Bobby's tiny apartment, taking John with her.

Mimi went through the roof. She took the bus over to Julia's, where she found the apartment was so small that John slept with Julia and Bobby in their bed. Mimi called in social services, who insisted John stay with Mimi until Julia and Bobby moved into a bigger place.

With no children of their own, Mimi and her husband, George, had plenty of room in "Mendips," their gracious, three-bedroom house. They put John in the small room next to their own bedroom.

Julia didn't seem to be in a hurry to find a bigger place. Mimi was sure it was because no man would want another man's child around.

One day Freddie appeared at Mimi's door. He'd come for his son. Freddie gathered up John's clothes, and left with him. Mimi was frantic. She found Julia and told her what had happened. Julia promised she'd somehow locate them.

Freddie took John to the seaside resort of Blackpool, where they stayed with a friend of Freddie's while he figured out what to do next. Needing to make some money, Freddie parked John with his brother Sydney and his wife Madge and went down to Southampton to sell nylons on the black market. Sydney and Madge were entranced with John and said they'd like to adopt him. But Freddie had other plans. He took John back to Blackpool and looked into emigrating with him to New Zealand.

On Saturday, July 22, 1946, Julia showed up in Blackpool and confronted Freddie. She wanted John back. They argued back and forth, and Freddie finally shouted for John, who ran in from the next room. Freddie told John he had to make a choice: Stay with him or go with Julia.

John chose Freddie. Julia began to cry, and asked again.

It was an agonizing decision. For the second time, John chose his father.

Freddie stepped in. "That's enough, Julia," he said sharply. "You've had your answer. Leave him alone." Julia reluctantly left and headed up the street.

John was shattered. He suddenly changed his mind, and ran after his mother, crying.

Julia was relieved and thrilled. She jumped on the train with John, hurried back to Liverpool, and delivered John back to Mimi and George.

ABOVE: *John, around age five.*

Mimi was determined to create a stable home for John. He'd lived the first years of his life in the constant dread and chaos of the war, his father gone, his mother often relinquishing his care to others. Mimi carefully inspected the nearby schools and enrolled him in Dovedale Primary School.

She insisted John speak proper English, not rough, guttural Scouse, and she found the most effective discipline was to ignore him when she was angry. But she adored him, and John knew it. She always made sure she was home when he came back from school, and never once left the house in the evening. One day John asked Mimi why he didn't call *her* "Mummy." "Well— you couldn't very well have *two* Mummies, could you?" That seemed to satisfy him.

George was a softer touch. John would leave notes under his pillow: *"Dear George, will you wash me tonight and not Mimi?"* or *"Dear George, will you take me to Woolton Pictures?"* The two of them would slip off to the movie theater to see cowboy films from America or swashbuckling adventure films. It made Mimi jealous when they went off without her. Sometimes when Mimi sent John to his room for misbehaving, she'd find George creeping upstairs with John's favorite comic, *Beano*, and a chocolate bar. "George, you're ruining him," she'd say sternly. "We can't have two fools in the house. One's enough."

What Mimi and John shared was a love of books. "His mind was going the whole time, and it was either drawing, or writing poetry, or reading," she said. "He was a great reader. It was always books, books, books." Richmal Crompton's Just William series about a mischievous boy was one of John's favorites. William stole food from the pantry when he was hungry, ran away from home when he felt put upon, and, with his friends the Outlaw Gang, acted out parts from movies and books, always with disastrous results for those around him. With burnt cork rubbed on his face and turkey feathers in his hair, William became Indian Chief "Red Hand." He lit a fire in a remote corner of the garden where he cooked up "palefaces" and ate them.

Creating a gang like William's, John rounded up several neighborhood friends—Ivan Vaughan, a budding bookworm; Nigel Walley, whose father was a police sergeant; and Pete Shotton, a rambunctious boy with an angelic face—and masterminded their games. For "cowboys and Indians" John would dress up as an Indian with lipstick "war paint" on his face and pheasant feathers in his hair. He insisted the other boys be cowboys. In John's version, the cowboys always lost. "And when he said they were dead, they were dead," Mimi said. When they didn't do it his way, he'd yell, "Pretend properly!"

John asked Mimi about his parents, but she gave him only the barest details, saying they had fallen out of love and his father was so brokenhearted he couldn't face coming back to Liverpool. John soon forgot his father, saying later, "It was like he was dead." But he had very different feelings about his mother, who lived nearby in the new postwar housing with Bobby and their two young daughters, Julia and Jacqui. His mother would breeze in to Mendips to laugh and gossip with Mimi and to see John. "My feeling never died off for her," said John. "I often thought about her."

In the evenings, John often listened to the radio with Mimi and George. Like most families of the time, they didn't have a television. At 6:45 a thriller series, *Dick Barton, Special Agent*, came on. When Dick Barton was in trouble, John couldn't sit still. Caught up in the terrifying adventure, his face would go white as a sheet. Another of his favorites was *The Goon Show*,

Summer 1949: John with his mother, Julia Lennon.

not for the tense drama, but the hilarity. Three comedians, Peter Sellers, Harry Secombe, and Spike Milligan, caught up in ludicrous plots, made puns and spun off nonsensical jokes in a variety of accents, accompanied by wild sound effects. "Excuse my dirty hands, but I've just been washing my face," was one off-the-cuff remark. "Come in, sit down. Have a gorilla," went another. "No thanks, I'm trying to give them up."

Each episode featured an inventive jazz harmonica player, Max Geldray. George, quick to pick up on John's keen interest, bought him an inexpensive harmonica. John carried it with him everywhere, constantly pulling it out of his pocket and teaching himself simple tunes.

Over summer vacation, John and his cousin Leila took the bus up to Scotland to visit their aunt Mater's farm. On the long ride north, John played his harmonica the whole way. The bus driver promised John a better harmonica if he came back in the morning. John was so excited he couldn't stop talking about it all evening. First thing in the morning, he was back at the bus station to collect his new harmonica.

At Dovedale, art quickly became his favorite subject. Before he'd been there long, his drawings were put up in the hallway exhibitions. He read voraciously, and as soon as he finished a book, for instance *The Wind in the Willows*, he wanted to relive it all over again. He bullied and cajoled other boys at the school into acting out what he'd just read. The others were always in awe of him: He had a sharp tongue and was quick with his fists. If there was a fight on the playground he was sure to be involved in it.

Introduced to Lewis Carroll's *Alice in Wonderland* and *Through the Looking Glass*, John quickly memorized Carroll's surrealistic poem "Jabberwocky":

'Twas brillig, and the slithy toves
Did gyre and gimble in the wabe:
All mimsy were the borogoves
And the mome raths outgrabe.

ABOVE: John's class photo from 1951-52, taken during his last year at Dovedale Primary School.
LEFT: A 1951 school trip to the Isle of Man. John is in the front row, second from left. With his hand on John's shoulder is Peter Sissons, and to the right of John are Jimmy Tarbuck, Mike Hill (in back row), and Ivan Vaughan.

He was delighted by the way Carroll put two words together to come up with a new word: "Slithy" was made of lithe and slimy; "mimsy" from miserable and flimsy. He drew all the characters in *Alice in Wonderland* and *Through the Looking Glass*, and wrote poems styled after "Jabberwocky." Entranced by the Just William stories, he wrote his own versions, putting himself in William's place. Fed by books and radio, his extraordinary talent to imagine poured out of him. "I used to *live* Alice and Just William," he said later.

At school they discovered John was profoundly nearsighted—he could only see up close, and not far away. Mimi took him to get free wire-frame glasses from the National Health Service. John loathed his glasses and rarely wore them. The last thing he could afford was to look like a sissy.

At Sunday school, John's friend Pete figured out a weak chink in John's tough exterior. When the students were asked to recite their names, John muttered his full name . . . John Winston Lennon. Pete immediately nicknamed him Winnie and tormented him by calling him Winnie in front of others. One day Pete was walking home alone when John jumped out from behind a clump of trees. "Listen you," he said. "If you keep calling me Winnie, I'm going to have to smash you up."

John knocked Pete to the ground and straddled him. After Pete swore he'd never call him Winnie again, John let him up. Pete scuttled about ten yards away, turned around, and yelled, "Winnie, Winnie, Winnie, Winnie, Winnie!"

John was boiling with anger. Then he suddenly broke into a grin. They became inseparable. John linked their two names together, dubbing them "Shennon and Lotten."

It suited fast-talking, tough, independent John to have a loyal partner who could stand up to him.

John evened the score over "Winnie" by coming up with a nickname for Pete, calling him "Peen." Only Pete knew it was short for penis, concocted in honor of skinny Pete's flushed face and white-blond hair. "A penis is thin and long," said Pete later, "with a red head and has white stuff coming out of the top—just like me." John's tongue was merciless, even with his friends.

Tearing around the neighborhood on their bikes, John led Pete and the rest of his gang into mischief. At the West Allerton bridge, they lobbed chunks of dirt and grass at the trains passing below. In a forbidden, overgrown field with a deep pond, they built a raft and punted across. Before heading home they dried their wet, muddy clothes in front of a bonfire started with matches filched from the kitchen.

But no matter how tough John acted, a profound struggle was going on inside him. "I just see and hear *differently* from other people," he said later. "And there is no way of explaining it."

One day when he was eight or nine he walked into the kitchen and told Mimi, "I've just seen God."

Mimi asked him what God was doing.

"Oh, just sitting by the fire," John answered.

In her practical way, Mimi replied, "I expect he was feeling a bit chilly."

As deeply as Mimi loved John, she was clueless about his deeper feelings. To her, he was "happy as the day was long."

Inside, John was in turmoil. "I was always seeing things in a hallucinatory way that always saw beyond the mask," he said. It made him feel alone and afraid. "Neither my auntie nor my friends nor anybody could *ever* see it! And it's very, very scary."

In his last year at Dovedale, John sailed through the rigorous "eleven-plus" exam, which decided whether he would go on to a vocational or academic school. Along with Pete Shotton, he was sent to Quarry Bank School, an austere, ivy-covered campus a mile away. John was dismayed as he surveyed the hundreds of new boys at Quarry Bank, most of them older, bigger, and stronger. "Christ," he thought, "I'll have to fight all my way through this lot, having just made it at Dovedale."

Winston Churchill, affectionately called "Winnie" by the British public. John's mother Julia was so inspired by his leadership during the war she gave John the middle name of Winston, much to his later embarrassment. John claimed that he had read Churchill's entire collected works.

2

ROCK'N'ROLL

1952-1956

"Rock'n'roll was real—everything else was unreal.
To me it got through—it was the only thing to get through to me
out of all the things that were happening when I was fifteen."

IN HIS FIRST Quarry Bank fight John did a lot of swearing and shouting and threw a quick punch, but he lost. It wasn't a good beginning. "I wanted to be the leader," John said. "It seemed more attractive than just being one of the toffees. I wanted everybody to do what I told them to do, to laugh at my jokes and let me be the boss."

Quarry Bank preferred the toffees, staunchly upholding its reputation of turning out well-educated, dependable young members of the British empire. The teachers, dressed in scholarly black gowns, insisted on rigid adherence to discipline and learning. Every student wore a regulation tie and black blazer, with an embroidered patch bearing the school's Latin motto: *Ex hoc metallo virtutem* (From this rough metal we forge virtue).

Forging virtue from the "rough metal" of a group of teenage boys was not a subtle job. The students were divided into "houses" according to where they lived. John and Pete were put in Woolton House. Misbehavior resulted in black marks from the housemaster. Enough

LEFT: John and his older cousin Stanley Parkes with John's new bike, standing in front of Mendips.
TOP: The Quarry Bank school badge that John wore on his school uniform.

black marks and they would be sent to the dreaded headmaster, who kept a punishment book. Corporal punishment—being struck across the hands, legs, or butt with a cane—was the norm.

Put in the top A stream, John began the school year studiously doing his homework, as he had done at Dovedale. But he couldn't resist rebelling against the strict atmosphere. He and Pete figured out how to rig the portable blackboards so they would collapse the minute the teacher began writing on them, filled their bike pumps with ink to squirt at others on the playground, and hid alarm clocks in their school satchels set to go off in the middle of a lesson. If Pete was asked to stand in front of the class, John would hold up a drawing for Pete to see when the teacher wasn't looking, forcing Pete into a giggling fit.

Their black marks piled up, and they were sent down to the headmaster's study. E. R. Taylor was a tall, imposing man they had seen only occasionally, striding through the halls, his black gown flapping. John went in first, leaving Pete in the corridor outside nervously waiting his turn. He could hear the headmaster's raised voice through the wall, then the heavy thwack of the cane hitting John's backside.

John emerged on his hands and knees, groaning terribly. Pete, well aware that caning was painful, was still shocked at how terrible John looked. Then John cracked a grin, and Pete realized that once John was out of sight of the headmaster, he'd dropped down on all fours to scare him. Pete burst into nervous giggles just as he was called into the headmaster's study.

"If you think this is funny, Shotton," he yelled, "I'll show you what's funny! Bend over that chair." Pete had been caned before, but this was the worst caning of his life.

To Pete's immense relief, the next time they were sent to the headmaster's study, the deputy head was there. He was an old, balding geography teacher known for being absentminded. He told John and Pete to stand behind him while he looked up their names in the punishment book.

As he searched through the book, John reached forward and tickled the last few hairs on the teacher's bald head. Thinking it was a fly, the deputy head distractedly rubbed his hand across his head. As soon as he dropped his hand, John went after him again.

Pete faked a coughing fit to cover up the laughter threatening to erupt out of him. John thought his joke was so funny he couldn't control himself and peed in his pants. Pee dripped from the edge of his shorts and trickled onto the floor, causing the headmaster to raise his head and look around. "What's that, what's that?" he said. "I think the roof's leaking, sir," John replied. It wasn't even raining.

In their 1955 Quarry Bank School class photo, fourteen-year-old John (second row, second from left) stands next to Pete Shotton, nicknamed "Snowball" when he was born for his white-blond hair.

John continued to defy the school rules, and was caned for talking back to his teachers, swearing, gambling on the playing field, and "skiving off" school. It finally resulted in a change in his behavior: He quit telling the truth. At Dovedale he'd been honest, owning up to what he'd done. But now he saw it just got him in further trouble.

John poured his interests and talents into an exercise book he dubbed the "Daily Howl." He filled the book with weather reports, made-up news stories, and weird, offbeat drawings. Sometimes he used a witty, backtracking doubletalk. "Our late editor is dead, he died of death, which killed him. His wife married again, the day he died, and sold his possessions which he owned." He did wickedly funny caricatures of his teachers, and irreverent cartoons. In one, he drew a man and woman in bed. In the next frame they were standing before a minister, the groom's eyes bugging out as he looked at what the woman held in her arms—a newborn baby. John titled the sketch "I do." His drawings were filled with deformities and handicaps. Eyes bulged, hands became claws, a body might have only one leg and two heads.

Though he rarely read what was assigned in class, he devoured everything Mimi had on her shelves, from her Book of the Month Club selections to Balzac and Fitzgerald. Mimi, strict, sensible, and orderly, would never have wanted bizarre people around the house, but she loved to read about artistic people like Oscar Wilde and Vincent van Gogh.

At twelve or thirteen, acutely aware of his appearance, John would stare at himself in the bathroom mirror. "I would find myself seeing these hallucinatory images of my face changing, becoming cosmic and complete," he related later. "I would start trancing out and the eyes would get bigger and the room would vanish."

Books were his lifeline. "The only contact I had was reading something about Oscar Wilde or Dylan Thomas or Vincent van Gogh—of the suffering they went through because of their vision. They were *seeing* and being tortured by society for trying to express what they were."

"Surrealism had a great effect on me," he said, "because then I realized that the imagery in my mind wasn't insanity—that if it was insane, then I belonged to an exclusive club that sees the world in those terms."

After school, John was kingpin of his gang. He and Pete would flee the restraints of Quarry Bank to meet up with Nigel and Ivan, who'd been sent off to other schools. They careened around town on bikes, kicking up trouble and fun. Thanks to a girl in his neighborhood, John had a vast repertoire of dirty jokes, and he recounted them to the others with relish. In the shops, he'd innocently ask a clerk if he could see something on a high shelf, then stuff his pockets with toffees and chocolates as soon as the clerk turned his back. In the tobacco shops, John bought cigarettes for two pence each or stole handfuls, and sold them to other kids. "The sort of gang I led went in for things like shoplifting and pulling girls' knickers down," John admitted. Rather than pay to ride the tram, John would swing onto the back bumper, terrified the whole time he'd fall off. But fear only seemed to make him act more outrageously.

An 1882 engraving of Oscar Wilde (1854–1900), reflecting his proclivity for being in the hot seat. Deliberately provocative and a flamboyant dresser, Wilde was controversial in Victorian England.

THE RED HOT STOVE.

CAN STAND IT IF YOU CAN

"John was always the leader," Nigel said. "He was always the one to dare you. He never cared what he said or did. He'd think nothing of putting a brick through the glass in a street lamp."

The only friend Mimi approved of was Nigel, because his father was a police sergeant. Mimi thought he would be a good influence on John. But the influence went the other way. "John used to look after me," Nigel said. "Whatever he told me to do, I'd do it."

In June 1955, while John and his cousin Leila were in Scotland, Uncle George suddenly collapsed and died of a liver hemorrhage. No one told John and Leila. When they returned to Mendips, Mimi was in the kitchen, trying to prepare supper, crying over the carrots. John didn't know what to do, or what to say. He and Leila slipped upstairs to his room, where their feelings exploded in hysterical laughter. "We just laughed and laughed," said John later. "I felt very guilty afterwards."

By the fall of 1955, John and Pete had been demoted to the C stream at school. But it didn't make any difference. Life was happening after school and on the weekends. Another boy from Woolton House, Rod Davis, joined them. Mimi insisted that Rod, like all of John's friends, walk down the driveway and knock on the back kitchen door. Despite being a studious A-stream student, Rod was nervous around Mimi. "She was very strait-laced," Rod said. He was always careful of his manners around her.

It was far more fun to go to the latest movie, or climb the wall surrounding the Salvation Army girls' home at Strawberry Field, and disappear into the thick shrubbery full of rabbits and birds. Some days they raced over to Calderstones Park on their bikes, and perched on a gentle slope to talk, smoke, and watch the girls walk by. John, singing or playing his harmonica, led the gang in renditions of the latest popular tunes on BBC radio, like Johnnie Ray's "The Little White Cloud That Cried."

John with his cousin Leila and Uncle George. John's dog, Sally, is sitting by George's legs.

Sex kitten Brigitte Bardot, John's dream girl.

Sometimes they'd abandon their music and girl-watching and sneak into the bushes. Well-hidden in the foliage, they'd titillate themselves by fantasizing about the various sex kittens they were enamored of. John was unswervingly devoted to blonde, buxom Brigitte Bardot. At home he put posters of her up on his wall, even taping her life-size image on the ceiling over his bed.

Pete had a small black-and-white television, and they all piled into his living room to watch the latest American shows: *Highway Patrol*, *Dragnet*, and *The Whirlybirds*. Fascinated by the excitement of cops, cars, and helicopters chasing around sun-drenched Los Angeles, Pete thought the United States was "a futuristic paradise of fast cars, fast food, fast money, and fast women—a society infinitely more permissive and exciting than our own."

America's heady freedom reached them in another way: Radio Luxembourg. Late at night, they'd fiddle with the radio dial, straining their ears through the crackling static to hear the station's distinctive shows in English coming all the way from the tiny European principality of Luxembourg. Unlike the staid, family-oriented BBC programming, Radio Luxembourg featured a jam-packed evening of popular music. There was even a syndicated show, *Saturday Night Jamboree*, which featured black rhythm and blues by the original artists. Through the static, John heard the recklessness of Chuck Berry's "Maybellene," and the exuberance of Fats Domino's "Ain't That a Shame." A few white musicians slipped across the color barrier: Bill Haley grabbed the beat of black music and scored a hit with "Shake, Rattle and Roll."

Hollywood smelled money and jumped in with *Blackboard Jungle* in 1955. As gritty black-and-white shots of an American inner-city high school filled the screen, a drumbeat throbbed through the theater, launching Bill Haley's opening song, "Rock Around the Clock" over the opening credits. In the film, two tough, streetwise teens struggled for control of the class, the street, and their own futures. Though the setting was wildly different from John's own austere school, the issues of power, violence, and a fierce resentment of authority were uncannily similar to those in his life.

Well before he saw it, John heard about the next film with Bill Haley, titled simply *Rock Around the Clock*. Teenagers were going wild in movie theaters, jumping up to dance in the aisles. Boys took their flick knives out and slashed the upholstery, rocked the chairs free of their bolts, and threw them around the room. In nearby Manchester, authorities turned fire hoses on them. John eagerly headed off to see the film. To his immense disappointment, nobody tore up the Liverpool theater. But there was one thing wrong with the song, too: the singer. Bill Haley was pudgy, married, and staggeringly unsexy.

The great lyricist Chuck Berry, doing one of his trademark guitar licks.

Bill Haley's record Shake, Rattle and Roll *sold a million copies.*

ABOVE: *Jitterbugging in a "juke joint" in Clarksdale on the Mississippi Delta.* RIGHT: *Alan Freed, the first disc jockey and concert producer of rock'n'roll, at a live taping of his Moondog Show.*

By the end of the spring school term in 1956, John's record was dismal. His marks were poor, the teachers comments often scathing: "He is so fond of obtaining a cheap laugh in class that he has little time left for serious concentration," wrote his French teacher. "Still lazy," wrote another. Most damning of all was his math teacher's comment: "He is certainly on the road to failure if this goes on."

He was about to find salvation.

In America, whites had long disdained what they called "race music"—music by black artists recorded by major labels exclusively for black audiences. But in strictly segregated Memphis a Southern white man, Sam Phillips, loved the power of black rhythm and blues. Despite the derision of his friends, he built a small studio and recorded local blues musicians. He knew exactly what he was looking for. "I wanted something *ugly*. Ugly and honest. I knew that these people were disenfranchised. They were politically disenfranchised and economically disenfranchised, and to tell the truth, they were musically disenfranchised."

Phillips heard about an odd thing happening in record stores. Flush with money in the wealthy, postwar economy of the early 1950s, some white teenagers were buying "race music." Even those who wouldn't be caught dead buying a record by a black artist were listening to rhythm and blues on the radio. In Cleveland, disc jockey Alan Freed had inaugurated *The Moondog Show* in 1951. His program captivated mainly a young black audience, but quickly attracted white listeners as well. Freed coined the term "rock'n'roll" to describe the music

he was playing, and in 1954, moved his highly successful show to WINS in New York City.

"I knew that for black music to come to its rightful place in this country," Phillips said, "we had to have some white singers come over and do black music—not copy it, not change, not sweeten it. Just *do* it." He had an intuitive grasp of the complexities of prejudice and commerce. He said to his assistant, "If I could find a white man with a Negro sound I could make a billion dollars."

That man walked into his homemade recording studio in the spring of 1954. His name was Elvis Presley. Phillips recorded two of his songs, but wasn't particularly impressed. Phillips told Elvis to work with two of his friends, an electric guitar player and a bassist, and come back in a couple of weeks. They'd try again.

On July 5, 1954, Elvis came back with the two musicians. They were off to a slow start until Elvis launched into "That's All Right, Mama," by black bluesman Arthur Crudup. Suddenly Elvis cut loose and started moving around the studio like a red-hot gospel singer. The musicians started rocking along. "What the hell are you doing?" Phillips asked. The musicians couldn't say. "Well, find out real quick and don't lose it," Phillips replied. He caught it on tape and made it into a record.

Phillips's instincts were right. The world was hungry for Elvis: the flashpoint of synergy between black rhythm and blues and fledgling rock'n'roll. He was a good-looking, sneering young white man with sexy moves and an unforgettable voice for belting out songs.

In 1956, when John was fifteen years old, he heard Elvis's worldwide release, "Heartbreak Hotel," on Radio Luxembourg. "After that," he said, "nothing was the same for me."

To John and Pete, the wait between new Elvis songs seemed interminable, but new hits like "Blue Suede Shoes" and "Hound Dog" rolled out across the airwaves every few months. By late autumn of 1956, when John was in his final year at Quarry Bank, the first Elvis film, *Love Me Tender,* was released in theaters around the world. John joined hundreds of other teenagers packing the Gaumont Cinema for special matinees.

Elvis was spectacular. His voice, sultry and resonant, poured out of him. Tall and broad-shouldered, he wore outrageous clothes, long sideburns, his dark hair arrogantly swept back. He took over the stage like he owned it, hips gyrating, thighs shaking, snapping up on his toes to deliver a note. He was sexual, sensual, rude, and the best thing to happen in years. When

Elvis Presley, nicknamed "Elvis the Pelvis" because of his wild hip gyrations as he sang.

Elvis came on the screen, the girls gasped and cried and screamed in delight. John, like thousands of other boys, began to dress, swagger, and sneer with as much Elvis-like bravado as he could manage.

It didn't wash with Aunt Mimi. "It was Elvis Presley all day long," she complained. "I got very tired of him talking about this new singer." John couldn't care less what Mimi thought. She was just like other parents and teachers, watching in horror as rock'n'roll burst into the limelight, obscene and vulgar, corrupting their teenagers.

Abandoning any pretense of doing homework in the evenings, John sketched cartoons and scribbled out poetry, leaving crumpled-up scraps of paper all over the floor. When Mimi nagged him, he shot back, "You ought to pick these up, Mimi, because I'm going to be famous one day and they'll be worth something." He put up a poster of Elvis in his room and ordered Mimi to stay out. He and Mimi fought constantly.

John found an unexpected ally—his mother. Though he called Mimi "Aunt" and Julia "Mummy," their roles were exactly opposite. Mimi was desperately trying to steer John into a responsible adulthood; Julia offered John the free-spirited fun of a young aunt or older sister. Rather than just see her at Mendips under Mimi's watchful eye, he began hopping on the bus to her house.

Unlike Mimi and his teachers with their dire warnings, Julia understood John's rebellious streak—it was just like hers. Instead of properly discouraging him, she encouraged him. One weekday, John took Pete over to Julia's. She fed them cake and Coca-Cola and asked why they weren't in school. When John admitted they were cutting, she just laughed. "Well, it's lovely to see you both," she said. "Don't worry about school, don't worry about a thing. Everything's going to work out fine." John knew she wouldn't report him to Quarry Bank, or even mention it to Mimi.

Best of all, Julia shared his new obsession—she loved rock'n'roll. Her boyfriend Bobby had rigged up speakers in every room of their house and spent hours searching out new records for her. One day he came home with "Heartbreak Hotel."

"Is this the one you wanted?" he asked.

In reply, Julia flung her arms around his neck. They put the record on, dancing to it so wildly they lost their balance, laughing as they fell over.

When John visited, Julia would put rock'n'roll songs on her wind-up record player. She and John sang along and danced around the living room.

A group of John's friends on a school trip to Holland where Mike Hill bought the record of Little Richard's "Long Tall Sally." From left, Mike Hill, Pete Shotton, Mike Rice, Mr. Burnett (the teacher), and Don Beattie.

John was also able to listen to records at his friend Mike Hill's house. In April, Mike had tantalized John, saying the new American record he'd just bought on a school trip to Amsterdam was by a singer "better than Elvis." The record wasn't even for sale in Britain. John, along with Pete and another friend, Don Beattie, cycled over to Mike's house at lunchtime to listen to Little Richard's "Long Tall Sally." When John heard it, he was speechless. The others all noticed: John was never speechless.

"Both of us were loath to admit," said Pete, "that this caterwauling colored boy was every bit as electrifying as 'our' Elvis." But "Long Tall Sally" crumbled John's exclusive allegiance. He soon ranked Little Richard with Elvis and thought the singer was "so great I couldn't speak. . . . How could they be happening in my life, *both* of them?"

For the next year and a half, John and Pete frequently snuck away from school and spent their lunch hour at Mike's, eating fish and chips, playing poker, three-card brag or pontoon, smoking cigarettes, and listening to records.

Little Richard, famous for his screaming vocals, flamboyant piano playing, and outrageous showmanship.

Despite his fascination with rock'n'roll, John had no aspirations to perform. Rock'n'roll stars were glamorous, with expensive equipment. And black or white, every one of them was American. It was all part of the mesmerizing, thoroughly unattainable American dream.

An Englishman, Lonnie Donegan, changed everything. He made the dream possible when his recording of black bluesman Leadbelly's "Rock Island Line" flew straight up the charts in 1956. Donegan took American folk songs and Southern blues and played them as "skiffle," a late-1920s American term for music made by people with little money for instruments.

Donegan's basic, three-chord style was amazingly easy to learn. A cheap acoustic guitar would be backed up by a couple of homemade instruments: a washboard strummed with a thimble provided rhythm; a cord held tautly between a cut-off broom handle and an old tea chest substituted for an upright bass. A banjo and drums could be thrown in, but they weren't necessary. A skiffle craze struck Britain. In Liverpool, teenage boys formed and reformed into loose, impromptu skiffle groups.

At Quarry Bank, a new headmaster, Mr. Pobjoy, had taken over. He and John met when John was sent down to his office for punishment. Pobjoy, young and inexperienced, did what was expected of him: He caned John. But he didn't think caning made any difference in John's or anyone's behavior, and he quickly did away with it. Pobjoy—by now christened "Popeye"—tried a new tack. He wanted to get through to John, and asked him what his favorite activities were. John answered honestly: "Salmon fishing, writing poetry, painting, drawing, poster design and skiffle."

John finally had an ambition: He wanted to learn to *perform* music, not just listen. He had no guitar, but Julia played a mother-of-pearl banjo that had belonged to her grandfather. She sat patiently with him as he struggled to learn the fingering to the hit "That'll Be the Day" by Buddy Holly, then slowed down the record so he could scribble out the words.

Skiffle overshadowed all John's other interests. Not content with playing Julia's banjo, he scraped together the money to send away for a cheap guitar, the Gallotone Champion. Inside it was labeled, "Guaranteed not to split." When it came, neither he nor Julia had a clue how to play it. Julia tuned the top four strings like a banjo and left the bottom two slack.

Mimi worried herself sick about John's new interests and his poor attitude at home and at school. She'd yell up the stairs at John, "We're going to have law and order!" It didn't work. John took to spending the night—sometimes the whole weekend—at Julia's, listening to records and practicing his new guitar.

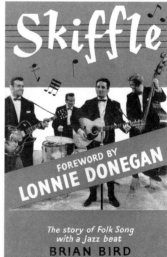

Lonnie Donegan's popularization of skiffle led to guitar sales in Britain shooting up from 5,000 in 1950 to 250,000 in 1957.

31

3

TWO OF US

1957

"It went through my head that I'd have to keep him in line if I let him join."

JOHN WASN'T THE only one of his gang who was bitten by the skiffle craze. Rod bought a banjo off his uncle, and John began working on Pete to join them. Pete, knowing he utterly lacked any musical skills, was unenthusiastic. But John badgered him until he dragged an old washboard out of his parents' garden shed and reluctantly learned to run a thimble up and down the corrugated metal. To complete their lineup, John and Pete got an old tea chest from Pete's mother and made it into a bass with a cord and broom handle. They talked a friend, Len Garry, into playing it. When he wasn't available, Nigel and Ivan took turns.

The group jammed into the old air-raid shelter in Pete's backyard. At first they stuck with Lonnie Donegan's easy chords and repetitive rhythm. "Rock Island Line" topped their repertoire, but they struggled through "Wabash Cannonball" and "Cumberland Gap" as well. The arched air raid shelter threw the sound back at them, amplifying the noise, covering up some of their worst mistakes.

The Quarry Men, July 6, 1957, at the garden fete just hours before John and Paul met. John is at the microphone. To the left of John is Rod Davis, and to the right are Pete Shotton and Len Garry.

Julia, always delighted to see John and his friends, encouraged them to bring their instruments over. The tiled walls of Julia's bathroom gave them great acoustics. They squeezed in, standing in the bathtub, perching on the toilet seat, pressed against the sink. Julia, with her infectious enthusiasm, joined them, drumming on the bottom of a pan or taking over the washboard. She taught them other popular hits: "Ramona" and "Wedding Bells Are Breaking Up That Old Gang of Mine."

John instinctively took the role of leader. The others let him. "First," said Rod practically, "he knew one more chord than the rest of us." He sang the lead vocals and left the others to join in the chorus. Different friends came and went, but John was always the one to decide if they were in or out. When he'd had enough of someone, he picked a fight and forced him out.

As they practiced, John thrashed at the strings of his guitar, sometimes snapping them.

He'd hand his guitar to Rod, who replaced the string, while John kept playing on Rod's banjo. John relied on a neighbor to tune his guitar, or asked his mother for help. Before long they added Elvis's "Jailhouse Rock" and "Blue Suede Shoes" to their repertoire, and a Liverpool sailors' song, "Maggie May."

John, in a sarcastic homage to a line in their school song, "Quarry Men, strong before our birth," named his group the Quarry Men. Soon they were good enough to play at friends' parties, church hall dances, and the skiffle contests springing up in ballrooms and youth clubs. One night Rod's father drove them over to the Locarno ballroom on the other side of town for a contest. While they were nervously waiting their turn, John smoked a cigarette, right down to a stub, then threw it down on the plush red carpeting and ground it out with his foot. Rod's shocked father said, "Surely you don't do that at home, John."

John just gave him a terrible look. He wasn't willing to behave himself around anyone. All that mattered was the music. It was loose and wild and sweaty, free of the constraints every-one was shoving at him.

Mimi wanted him to concentrate more on his schoolwork. But John kept at her, saying, "Let me get it out of my system, Mimi."

John practiced up in his room, hour after hour, day after day. Mimi, unable to stand the sound of his playing as it reverberated through the ceiling, banished him to the glassed-in porch at the front of the house. John discovered that the small room had wonderful acoustics. Mimi, always determined to get in the last word, chastised him for spending all his time practicing. "The guitar's all very well, John," she said, "but you'll never make a *living* out of it."

In the spring of 1957, John was sixteen and full of resentment when he sat down to take his "Ordinary" level exams during his last semester at Quarry Bank. For years it had been drummed into him just how important the O levels were: Those who failed left school and looked for work. Asked to draw a travel scene for his art exam, John derisively penned in a hunchback covered with warts.

Despite his caustic attitude, John realized he had better figure out how to earn a living. He

This 1957 class photo was taken in John's last year at Quarry Bank. John (third row down, five in from the left) is flanked by friends: to the left of John is Pete Shotton; to the right are Don Beattie and Mike Hill.

brought home an older boy who waited tables at sea. "This boy's got *pots* of money," John whispered to Mimi. "Ha!" said Mimi. "A fine ambition!"

Without waiting for John's exam results, Pobjoy called Mimi into his office. What, he asked, was she going to do with him? Mimi bristled. "What are *you* going to do with him?" she asked. "You've had him five years."

Pobjoy believed John deserved a chance to make something of himself, and wrote him a letter of recommendation for the Liverpool Art School. Though John failed all his O levels, the art college accepted him. He was promised a place in the fall, starting shortly before his seventeenth birthday.

The Quarry Men hadn't played many recent gigs when Pete's mother arranged for them to play July 6, 1957, at the St. Peter's Parish Church garden fete—the big summer celebration in Woolton.

The day began inauspiciously for John. He carefully greased back his hair and put on a checked shirt and tight drainpipe trousers. When Mimi caught sight of him, she was furious to see him decked out like Elvis. She and John got into a terrible fight, shouting at each other until John slammed out of the house. Though John knew Mimi went to the garden fete every year, he didn't own up to her that he'd be there in his outrageous clothes, standing up onstage for the whole neighborhood to see, playing in his band.

By midday when John met up with Pete, the day was already warm. Though he was still underage, John managed to pick up several bottles of light ale and guzzle them down on their way. By the time they arrived, the church grounds were decorated with flags, balloons, and bunting. In the big white refreshment tents, women were putting together sandwiches and laying out homemade cakes.

Mimi arrived just before the Quarry Men started their first set. She was having a cup of tea in one of the tents when the band started up with a loud explosion of noise. Mimi followed as everyone poured out of the tent to the far field where the band was set up.

John caught sight of her as she walked toward the stage, openmouthed, staring at him. He quickly began busking, making up words to the song he was singing. "Mimi's

ABOVE: John's headmaster, William E. Pobjoy

The Quarry Men performed June 22, 1957, on Rosebery Street, Toxteth, Liverpool, from the back of a flatbed truck used to haul coal. Colin Hanton on drums, Eric Griffiths on guitar, John at the microphone, Len Garry on tea chest bass, Pete Shotton on washboard, and Rod Davis on banjo. This is the earliest known photo of John and the Quarry Men.

coming," he sang. "Oh, oh, Mimi's coming down the path. . . ." It was the first time Mimi had ever seen him playing with the Quarry Men. She couldn't believe her eyes. The band moved on to their other big numbers, "Railroad Bill," "Cumberland Gap," and "Maggie May."

While Mimi was still reeling, a friend of Ivan's, Paul McCartney, arrived on his bike. Paul was dressed to kill: He'd come to the garden fete hoping to pick up girls. His white sports jacket was shot through with metallic threads that sparkled in the sunlight, his black drainies were tight, his hair was carefully greased back in a "duck's arse."

Paul arrived in time to hear John singing the Del Vikings' recent hit, "Come Go with Me." Instead of singing the lyrics "Come go with me, don't let me pray beyond the sea,"

John threw in words from American rhythm and blues songs: "Come go with me, down to the penitentiary." Paul was fascinated, amazed that John was making up his own lyrics.

While the Liverpool City Police Department put its German shepherds through their obedience trials—the day's big attraction—John and the other Quarry Men moved their equipment to the empty church hall where they were scheduled to play for the evening dance. They sat on folding chairs in the hall, drinking beer and talking.

Ivan turned up with Paul, eager to introduce him to John. John regarded Paul warily, then Paul borrowed a guitar and whipped into Eddie Cochran's "Twenty Flight Rock." John was incredulous. The song was too difficult for the Quarry Men. John moved in close, drunkenly hanging over Paul's shoulder, eager to watch his fingering. Paul ripped through "Be-Bop-a-Lula" and a couple of his favorite Little Richard songs. To top it off, Paul tuned John's guitar, showed him a couple of chords, and wrote out all the lyrics to "Twenty Flight Rock."

John, used to making snap decisions, was faced with a dilemma. Though Paul was nearly two years younger, he had impressive musical skills. He even knew how to tune his guitar! Having him in the group would immeasurably improve their music. But John worried it might also threaten his leadership. "I half thought to myself, 'He's as good as me.' Now, I thought, if I take him on, what will happen? I'd been kingpin up to then."

John decided Paul was worth having in the group, but made no effort to seek him out. Pete ran into Paul a few weeks later and casually invited him to join. Paul said he'd like to— as soon as he got back from Scout camp.

While John had to scrounge for every scrap of music he learned, Paul's house was full of music. One of Paul's earliest memories was lying on the living room floor listening to his father, Jim McCartney, play the piano. In the late 1920s he'd formed the Jim Mac Jazz Band, swinging through show tunes on the piano and trumpet. In 1941 he'd married Mary Mohin, a

ABOVE, TOP: *Ivan Vaughan.* BOTTOM: *Paul McCartney. Both are thirteen years old.*

Paul McCartney, around age six, with his brother, Michael, sitting behind him.

nurse, and they'd had two sons, Paul, born June 18, 1942, and Michael, born January 7, 1944. Jim became a cotton salesman, but at family gatherings aunts, uncles, and cousins still clustered around his piano while he led them in family singalongs.

Jim shared his love of music with Paul and Michael. He'd point out the bass line in music playing on the radio and he taught them to sing harmony. On weekends he'd take them to brass band concerts in the park, captivating Paul. Paul learned to play the piano as his father had done, picking out tunes by ear.

Though Jim had left school at fourteen, he enjoyed doing the crossword puzzle every day and encouraged his sons to do them. If they didn't know a word or how to spell it, Jim sent them over to the family's George Newnes Encyclopedias to look it up.

Mary's job as a nurse-midwife entitled the family to an unusual privilege: their own telephone. When she received a call that someone was in labor, she'd pull on her uniform and cycle off on her bike, no matter what time it was or what the weather. Like many postwar women, she

Ten-year-old Paul McCartney, fourth from the left, ringing handbells in the Anglican Cathedral.

aspired to a better life for her children, insisting they work hard at school and speak the Queen's English, not Scouse like their working-class neighbors. Her guidance paid off. In 1953, Paul was one of four students at his school to go on to the rigorous Liverpool Institute, where he easily stayed at the top of the class.

In October 1954, his academic interest was suddenly punctured by a song on BBC radio, the Crew Cuts' "Sh-Boom." The song, originally recorded on March 15, 1954, by the black R&B/doo-wop group the Chords, had made it on to the American pop charts, introducing many whites to R&B music for the first time. The Crew Cuts, a clean-cut white quartet, were immediately hired by a large music company to record a "cover" version with a big-band arrangement. When the Crew Cuts performed at the Liverpool Empire the next year, Paul watched the show, then ran around to the stage door and waited for them to emerge, autograph book in hand.

In 1955 the McCartneys moved to government housing in Allerton, about a mile from John and Mimi. Their new row house at 20 Forthlin Road had a small front and back garden, with a toilet in the garden shed. Upstairs were three little bedrooms and a new modern luxury, an indoor bathroom.

For Paul's fourteenth birthday his father gave him a trumpet. But Elvis had just burst on the scene with "Heartbreak Hotel." Tingles ran up and down Paul's spine when he heard Elvis, eclipsing Paul's love of brass bands and show tunes. He traded in his trumpet for an acoustic Zenith guitar.

At first, Paul couldn't get anywhere on his new guitar. When he finally saw a picture of left-handed Slim Whitman holding his guitar, Paul realized being left-handed was his problem. He restrung his guitar, putting the thin high string, which is usually on the bottom, on the top, allowing him to hold the guitar backwards.

The comfortable security of Paul's life shattered four months after his birthday. His mother had been feeling pains in her breast for months but didn't mention it to the doctors she worked with. When the pain became debilitating she finally consulted a doctor. They did surgery, but it was too late: Mary had advanced breast cancer. The boys were taken to the hospital to see her. "They must have known she was dying," Paul said. "It turned out to be our last visit and it was terrible because there was blood on the sheets somewhere and seeing that, and your mother, it was like, 'Holy cow!' . . . But we didn't really know what was happening." In his room, Paul prayed night after night that she would somehow, miraculously, come back.

After Mary's death, Jim struggled to be both mother and father to his sons, giving them nurturance as well as discipline. He hated it that they had to come home to an empty house after school, especially in winter when they had to light the fire to warm the house. He gave them keys to let themselves in, but warned them not to bring friends home when he was not there.

Paul coped with his grief by playing his guitar. He spent hours hunched over his guitar with its upside-down strings, strumming with his left hand, working out simple chords with his right. He took his guitar with him everywhere, even to the toilet. As soon as Paul had a few rudimentary chords down, he began composing songs. One of his first was "I Lost My Little Girl," written shortly after his mother died.

Like John, he was completely bowled over by Elvis. "Every time I felt low I just put on an Elvis and I'd feel great, beautiful," he said. "I'd no idea how records were made and it was just magic."

In school, Paul's literature teacher, Alan Durband, told the class they'd be studying *The Canterbury Tales* by Chaucer. Paul struggled with the Middle English— "A povre wydwe, somdeel stape in age . . ."—until Durband gave them a translation. Paul was completely captivated by Chaucer's bawdy humor:

> *Dark was the night as pitch, as black as coal,*
> *And at the window out she put her hole,*
> *And Absalon, so fortune framed the farce,*
> *Put up his mouth and kissed her naked arse*
> *Most savorously before he knew of this.*
> *And back he started. Something was amiss;*
> *He knew quite well a woman has no beard,*
> *Yet something rough and hairy had appeared.*

They moved on to Shakespeare, and Paul was hooked. He began reading plays by Oscar Wilde, Tennessee Williams, and George Bernard Shaw, directing them in his mind. He haunted the local bookstores, searching out books by Dylan Thomas and John Steinbeck. "There was a bookshop you could go in and very easily nick them," he said. "Gerald Hoffnung's cartoons was the first book I stole." On weekends he'd take a book of poetry and ride the ferry across the Mersey River and back. He'd sit on a bench, watching people, jotting down what he saw. "I really fancied myself as an artist. I was preparing. I didn't know how the hell I was ever going to achieve it from my background. People didn't become this. But my mind was full of it, it was an intoxication."

The other boys at school teased him: Not only was he smart, but he was actually *interested* in art, music, and academics. "I was called a college pudding," he admitted. "Fucking college puddin' was what they said."

He did have another consuming interest: girls. With his big eyes, long lashes, and sweet

ABOVE: Paul's teacher, Alan Durband

looks, he made good time with the girls. He was one of the first in his class—only fifteen—when he went all the way for the first time. "I told everybody at school next day, of course," he said later. "I was a real squealer."

On Friday, October 18, 1957, Paul performed with the Quarry Men for the first time at the New Clubmoor Hall. After the dance Paul launched into a few of his own songs. John was fascinated. Black rock'n'rollers like Chuck Berry and Little Richard wrote their own material, but except for Buddy Holly, white rockers rarely did. Here was someone who shared John's love of words *and* music.

RIGHT: *Paul's class photo from the Liverpool Institute, March 1960. Paul is in the center.*
OVERLEAF: *The Quarry Men play New Clubmoor Hall, Liverpool, on November 23, 1957. From left: Colin Hanton, Paul McCartney, Len Garry, John Lennon, and Eric Griffiths.*

4

HOLD ON

1957–1958

"It was awful, like some dreadful film where they ask you if you're the victim's son and all that. It was absolutely the worst night of my life."

JOHN SHOWED UP for his first day at art college in a colored shirt and tight drainpipe pants. He was immediately estranged from the other students, who dressed in arty outfits: heavy duffel coats, black turtlenecks, and thick Shetland sweaters. Nor were they into his beloved rock'n'roll. They were jazz aficionados, lugging their portfolios down into candlelit jazz cellars for long, earnest discussions.

Whatever hopes John had of salvation in the classroom were smashed during the first week of art school. The students had to sign in every morning, and they all had to begin their art education with two years of set curriculum in general study, with classes in lettering, figure drawing, and perspective. John was disgusted by the amount of time they spent calculating the mathematical proportions of the letters of the alphabet. It felt as useless as high school math.

One teacher did get through to him, an abstract painter named Arthur Ballard. Ballard

---

John gave this photo to Mimi, calling it his come-hither look.

hated the constraints of the classroom and often taught his classes in a nearby pub called Ye Cracke. He'd have students pin their work up on the wall and encourage the others to discuss it. John turned in slapdash work and sat slumped in his seat, rarely participating. One day Ballard discovered John had left behind his notebook. It was full of caricatures of students and teachers, with wickedly funny descriptions. Ballard held the notebook up at the next discussion. "When I talk about interpretation, boy, *this* is the kind of thing I mean as well," he said. "*This* is the kind of thing I want you to be doing."

John did find some redeeming benefits to being an art student. For the first time, he was in school with both sexes. After class he could hang out at Ye Cracke or the Jacaranda coffee bar, drinking endless cups of coffee. Other students began to warily cluster around him, drawn by his presence, leery of his sharp, sarcastic humor. He soon had a girlfriend, and when that ended, another.

The biggest benefit was totally unexpected: The art college was just around the corner from the Liverpool Institute, so close in fact, that there was a shortcut between them next to the school kitchens. Paul snuck over at lunchtime to practice with John. They'd hang out in the cafeteria or slip into an unused classroom.

With Paul's father away at work till six, his house was available. After school, they'd jump on the bus to Paul's house, where they could work undisturbed. If they got hungry they'd fry eggs, heat up canned beans, dump them over toast, and wash it all down with hot cups of tea.

The small living room with its worn furniture

The McCartney house at 20 Forthlin Road, Allerton, Liverpool. Paul's father, an avid gardener, sent Paul and Michael out with buckets to collect horse manure from the streets. Though most people had bicycles and a few had cars, garbage was still picked up in horse-drawn carts.

The McCartney's living room, where John and Paul spent so much time writing songs and playing guitars. Among the earliest songs John wrote here with Paul were "One after 909" and an instrumental, never recorded, called "Winston's Walk."

and carpeting made of four runners sewn together was all theirs until six. Paul taught John the chords he knew, and showed him how to tune his guitar. Sitting across from each other, they practiced for hours at a time, eagerly discovering how to play more chords. Since Paul's guitar was strung upside-down to accommodate Paul's left-handedness, John carefully watched Paul's fingers as they formed a mirror image to his own. At home he would stare at himself in the mirror as he practiced, willing his fingers to repeat what he was learning.

Anything associated with playing rock'n'roll fascinated them. A few months before they met, a group called the Coasters had released "Searchin'." When John and Paul heard that a boy across town had the record, they took a bus to his house to listen and learn the words. When the owner wasn't looking, they swiped the record. Another time they were told about someone who knew a difficult chord they didn't know—B7. They knew E and A, but the last chord of the sequence, B7, had eluded them. They jumped on first one bus, then another, impatient to add it to their repertoire.

On the outside, John and Paul couldn't be more different. Paul was unfailingly polite to others, eager to please. He channeled all his feelings into music, carefully keeping everything hidden behind his charming smile. John, full of bravado and anger, couldn't understand it. In an unusually honest moment he asked Paul, "How can you sit there and act normal with your mother dead? If anything like that happened to me I'd go off me head."

Day after day they sat in Paul's living room, working together to write songs. John admired how Paul slipped from the piano to the guitar, picking out chords as they worked up the lyrics to a new song. They'd choose an idea, play with it, and whip out a song. Sometimes one of them would come up with the melody and words, and the other would write the eight-bar "bridge"—a transitional passage that linked two sections of the song. Whenever they came up with one they liked, Paul put the words down in a composition book. Under the title to each song he carefully wrote in that it was an original composition by Lennon-McCartney.

The book filled up with simple songs like "That's My Woman" and "Too Bad about Sorrows." Some of these early songs were good enough to be recorded later: "Hello Little Girl," "Love Me Do," and "One after 909." Without a tape recorder, they had no way of preserving the music they had done. They put each song to a quick test: If they couldn't remember it the next day, it was no good.

Though John didn't have the musical talent Paul did, he had something invaluable: an animal-like, angry desperation that fused with the spirit of rock'n'roll. It was the catalyst Paul needed, a bittersweet turbulence that complemented his more even-tempered nature.

Paul's father took an instant dislike to John in his tight pants, his aggressive attitude rolling off of him. "When John came round the house," Paul's brother Michael said, "it might just as well have been the Devil."

Mimi was equally sure Paul was a bad influence on John. Paul rode over to John's, leaned his bike against the fence, and knocked at the front door. Mimi instantly detected that Paul was from a lower class, and she didn't want John hanging out with him. When he came to

---

RIGHT: Mendips, at 251 Menlove Avenue, in the leafy village of Woolton, where John lived with his aunt Mimi. Paul and John rarely practiced in his room: When they sat side by side on his bed the necks of their guitars would bang into each other, and Mimi didn't like hearing them practice. They were banished to the glassed-in front porch (top), which fortunately had wonderful acoustics.

visit, now properly trained to knock on the back door, she'd call upstairs, "John, your little friend's here."

"She was the kind of woman who would put you down with a glint in her eye, with a smile," Paul said. "But she'd put you down all the same." But John's middle-class life impressed Paul: his large house called Mendips, the way he said "Aunt Mimi," rather than "Auntie Mimi," even the complete set of Winston Churchill's books in the living room, which John swore he'd read. John had it, so he could reject it. Paul wanted it.

While John and Paul were getting to know each other, skiffle's heady era was coming to an end as quickly as it had begun. Washboards were exchanged for snare drums, and talented tea-chest players moved on to bass guitars. Paul and John scraped together enough money to buy cheap electrical guitars, but couldn't afford amplifiers. John talked the school into buying a public address system so he could borrow the amps. There was also an ingenious solution being used all over England: By wiring the guitar into the back of a radio, the noise of the guitar blasted out of the radio speaker.

Pete still played with the band, but he'd never gotten over his discomfort with being onstage. One night the band played at a party on Smithdown Lane and got roaringly drunk afterwards. John and Pete sat cross-legged on the living room floor, surrounded by their instruments and empty beer bottles, laughing hysterically at each other's jokes. Suddenly John seized Pete's washboard and broke it over his head. Pete lay on the floor, the washboard frame around his neck, crying and laughing at the same time. He knew it meant his days as a Quarry Man were over. He was free to go to their gigs, sit in the audience, and enjoy the show.

Paul was eager to introduce John to a boy he knew from school, George Harrison. Paul swore George was incredible on the guitar—much better than either of them. Paul arranged for John and George to meet when the Quarry Men played in February 1958. George was small, gangly, and only fourteen, a year behind Paul in school. "It was too, too much," said John. "George looked even younger than Paul, and

George Harrison, age thirteen.

George Harrison with his first guitar, made in Holland by Egmond. It was their cheapest model, made for beginners. Steel strings helped the sound to carry farther and gave it a raw, hard edge.

Paul looked about ten, with his baby face." While they were all riding home on the nearly deserted upper level of the bus, George pulled out his guitar and played "Raunchy"—a tough, complicated piece. John couldn't help himself. He was impressed. He grudgingly invited George to join the band.

George's parents, Louise and Harold Harrison, had married in 1931, and George, born February 25, 1943, was their fourth child. The whole family scrunched into a small "two-up/two-down" house—two bedrooms upstairs and a living room and dining room downstairs with a tiny kitchen. The front door opened onto the pavement, and the only toilet was out back. When it was time for a bath, a zinc tub was hauled into the kitchen and filled with water they'd heated. When George was six, they moved to 25 Upton Green, with a third bedroom, indoor plumbing, and a small front garden.

George aced his eleven-plus exam and was sent on to the Liverpool Institute in 1954. Across town, John was in his fourth year at Quarry Bank. At school, George tried to fit in, but he hated people telling him what to do all day. He stared out the window, daydreaming, drawing guitars in his composition books. As long as he was quiet, the teachers left him alone. "I was just trying to be myself," George said. "They were trying to turn everybody into rows of little toffees." Soon he was cutting classes and sneaking out of school to smoke behind the old air raid shelter.

Even with Louise working at the greengrocer's to supplement Harold's bus driving job, there was only enough money for basics. To earn some cash, George took a Saturday job as a delivery boy for the local butcher. With his first money he bought pointy-toed blue suede "winkle-pickers" and colored shirts.

George was awed by John and the whole art college crowd. At lunchtime, he joined Paul and headed over to the art college to find John. They'd talk music while they ate, then break out their instruments and play. After school, George stood outside the art college. He'd scan the students, running after John when he saw him leaving. He loved John's lilac shirt and blue jeans and long sideburns. Flattered and embarrassed by George's flat-out adoration, John lit into him. George ignored John's insults or threw back his own. John liked people to come up against him, and warmed up to George. As they practiced together, he discovered that musically George was a kindred spirit. "Now there were three of us who thought the same," said John.

Knowing that Mimi wouldn't approve of George, John began working on her, saying what a nice, generous boy he was. George arrived at Mendips for the first time with his hair in a crewcut, wearing a bright pink shirt. Mimi promptly threw him out. Although she eventually let George come to Mendips, she remained disapproving of his thick Scouse accent and his Teddy boy clothes. Mimi was anxious about the rebellious Teddy boys' rowdy ways, which occasionally erupted into violence and vandalism.

Though John was in college, Mimi still felt she was responsible for shaping his character. In truth, they both had incredibly volatile natures. Pete Shotton was always surprised how unpredictable their fights were. One minute they'd be yelling and screaming at each other, the next minute they'd be laughing.

Underneath her tough, bossy exterior, Mimi was afraid she was losing John. As much as she adored him, she could see he was in danger of not pulling his life together. Her worst fear was that he would end up like his father. John reacted to her worried, angry lectures by storming out of the house for Julia's, swearing he was leaving for good.

Mimi called his bluff one weekend. When he returned from Julia's, his dog Sally was gone. Mimi had gotten rid of her, since John said he wasn't coming back.

Unlike Mimi with her reproving attitude, Julia loved to have John and his friends come over to visit and play their music. Paul joined the others squeezing into the bathroom. Julia especially had a soft spot for Paul, saying to John, "You must bring Paul home for something to eat. Poor lad, losing his mother."

Paul could tell John loved to visit his mother, but noticed that a feeling of sadness clung to John after they left. "Being John, he didn't admit to it much," Paul said, "unless it was a very quiet or drunken moment when he felt he could let his guard down."

Day after day John practiced the guitar, alone in the front hall at home, at Julia's, or with Paul and George at their homes. They went to see all the blues and rock'n'roll players who performed in Liverpool. They'd sit as close to the stage as possible, watching the

John's mother, Julia, in 1950, with her baby daughter Jacqui.

performers' fingers forming chords. New songs poured out of John and Paul, carefully recorded in Paul's notebook.

Bolstered by George's skilled guitar work and John and Paul's increasing repertoire of new songs, the Quarry Men played whenever they could. They wanted to cash in on some of the astonishing effect that Elvis had on girls, who screamed with delight when he came on the big screen at the movie theater. Picking up a girl after performing became a goal for John and Paul. If they were lucky enough to attract someone, they couldn't head home, since some adult was always there. They'd try to get off alone somewhere with the girl for a "knee-trembler" in an alleyway or behind someone's garden shed.

By the summer of 1958 John had made it through his first year of art college. On the evening of July 15, his friend Nigel dropped in at Mendips to visit John and found Julia and Mimi chatting by the front gate. Julia had stopped by for a cup of tea with Mimi and was on her way back home, where John was staying for the weekend. Nigel walked with Julia through the twilight toward the bus stop. Julia told him a new joke she'd just learned, then said good-bye and headed across busy Melrose Avenue. She crossed the first two lanes then disappeared into the hedge running down the middle of the road.

Moments later Nigel heard the squeal of brakes and spun around. An oncoming car veered toward the hedge and Julia's body hurtled through the air. From inside, Mimi heard the brakes and flew out of the house. Julia died instantly.

At Julia's house, Bobby and John were waiting, wondering why Julia was so late, when a police officer knocked at the door. He asked John if he was Julia's son, then told them she'd been hit by a car and killed.

At the hospital, Bobby went in to see Julia's body, but John refused. He couldn't bear to see his mother lying dead. After seeing Julia, Bobby broke down in John's arms. John didn't cry. He felt frozen inside.

Nigel was tormented by terrible guilt. If only he'd said just one more sentence to Julia, just a few words, perhaps she'd still be alive.

Everyone's despair was intensified when the driver, a drunk off-duty policeman, stood trial for reckless driving. Nigel testified, but because of his age, no one gave much credence to what he'd seen. Mimi was beside herself with anger and grief, shouting at the man as he was on the witness stand, threatening him with her walking stick. The driver was acquitted.

When art college started back again in the fall, John showed up—introspective, drinking heavily, lashing out with renewed cruelty. He spared no one. Pete watched John suffering, unable to help. One night—drunk as usual—John hurled taunts at a piano player named Reuben. "Creepy Jewboy," he yelled, "they should've stuck you in the ovens with the rest of 'em!" On the street, John ridiculed people with disabilities. He'd leer at people in wheelchairs as he passed them, accusing them of just trying to get out of the army. Late one night Pete got on a bus and discovered John sprawled out on a seat on the upper deck, drunk out of his mind. Pete roused him, carried him off the bus, and got him to bed at Mendips.

John came to school late, returned from lunch break drunk. He stayed in school only because it was better than getting a job. Sometimes he'd retreat up to the top of the main staircase and sit alone for hours. His teacher Arthur Ballard chanced upon him one day, and found him crying.

Paul understood what John was going through better than anyone else. "Now we were both in this; both losing our mothers," said Paul. "This was a bond for us, something of ours, a special thing." Though John seemed to have little interest in performing, he and Paul continued to get together to practice and write songs. As they sat together in John's bedroom one day, he came up with an idea they worked into a song, "I Call Your Name."

"What did he mean?" Paul wondered later. "'I call your name but you're not there.' Is it his mother? His father?" John wasn't looking for deep meanings in his lyrics. He was just trying to hold on.

5

MAKE SHOW!

1958-1961

"I was raised in Liverpool, but I grew up in Hamburg."

AT SCHOOL, ARTHUR Ballard was keeping his eye on another student just a few months older than John, Stuart Sutcliffe. Though shy and frail-looking, Stuart had enormous talent. He spent days at his easel, filling large canvases. Hours would pass and he wouldn't stop to eat or rest. John, impressed by Stuart's unique talent and drive, began to seek him out. They hung out at Ye Cracke or in Stuart's one-room apartment in a rundown part of the city crowded with artists. Stuart set up his easel in the middle of the room and threw a mattress on the floor underneath huge, dirty windows. Canvases were propped against the walls, and half-used tubes of paint tumbled off the mantel. It was a far cry from Mimi's orderly house and rigid rules.

Stuart and John ricocheted off each other, their fast, impatient minds spinning. Fascinated by John's music, Stuart ate lunch with Paul, George, and John, watched the Quarry Men practice, and came to their occasional performances. John, eager to get away from Mimi, began to spend the night at Stuart's. He and Stuart would stay up late, take apart Vicks inhalers, and stick the cardboard wick in water to get the speedy Benzedrine out of it. They'd

George, John, and Paul in 1961 behind Paul's house.

Stuart Sutcliffe, with his moody scowl and dark glasses looked like his idol, actor James Dean, who starred in the 1955 film Rebel without a Cause.

put rock'n'roll records on and paint together. Stuart encouraged John to go beyond the small, tight sketches he was so good at, pushing him to fill large canvases with loose abstracts. Rarely willing to trust other people's judgment, John felt differently about Stuart. "I looked up to Stu. I depended on him to tell me the truth," John said. "Stu would tell me if something was good and I'd believe him."

Unlike Stuart, who had little time for romance, John was always interested, but his temper and erratic behavior quickly drove his girlfriends away. Then an unlikely student fell for him.

Timid, conscientious, and prim-looking, Cynthia Powell was everything John wasn't. She lived with her mother in Hoylake, the posh suburbs across the Mersey River. She kept her hair in a modest perm, dressing in tweed skirts and twin-set sweaters. Despite herself, she found John fascinating.

Someone like Cynthia seemed completely unattainable to John. The best he could do was make fun of her. When he saw her come into class he'd yell out, "No dirty jokes, please—it's Cynthia."

She showed up early for lettering, their one class together, trying to figure out where John would sit so she could sit near him. In return for her trouble, he stole rulers, pencils, and erasers from her tidy collection. She thought his humor was sick, his drawings repulsive, but she couldn't stop admiring them and laughing. Several times Cynthia saw him lean up against his desk and quietly play his guitar. His face softened, his nervous aggression seemed to disappear. The tenderness under his rough exterior made him even more appealing.

When the school announced an afternoon dance, Cynthia was eager to attend. Students took up a collection of money for booze, found a record player, and crowded into a small room at the college. She was sure John wouldn't come to such a tame affair. When he showed up, her legs turned to jelly. She'd just gotten her composure back when he walked over and asked her to dance to the Teddy Bears' "To Know Him Is to Love Him." Cynthia was mortified and thrilled when she realized it was a slow dance. The other students looked at the two of them in amazement.

Afterwards Cynthia sat talking and laughing with John and the other art students in the crowded pub. It was clear to John she was infatuated with him. "I was triumphant, having picked her up," he said. "We had a drink then went back to Stu's flat, buying fish and chips on the way." Prim, modest Cynthia was so infatuated with John she made love with him that very first night.

Cynthia was far more refined and respectable than any girl John had been with before, her quiet composure alluring. John fell for her with complete abandon and could barely stand to have her out of his sight. They'd sit for hours in Ye Cracke, holding hands, staring into each other's eyes. Sometimes they cut class and went to the movies, just to be together in the warm, intimate darkness of the theater. John could even persuade her to tell her mother she was staying overnight with a girlfriend, and they'd have the exquisite, illicit pleasure of spending the night together at Stuart's.

When he wasn't with her, John poured out his love in notes scrawled in his cramped, impetuous handwriting: "I love you forever and ever isn't it great? I love you like guitars . . . I love you I need you don't go I love you."

It wasn't long before Cynthia realized she would take the full brunt of his unreasonable temper as well as his adoration. One minute they'd be getting along beautifully, then suddenly John would be in a white-hot fury. He'd accuse her of not loving him enough or being unfaithful. His possessiveness was overwhelming and filled her with dread. If she so much as talked to another man, John was consumed with jealousy, and if someone dared ask her to dance John was ready to beat him up. Cynthia pleaded with him to be reasonable, to consider his behavior. "He was so rough," Cynthia said. "He wouldn't give in."

He couldn't. "I was in a sort of blind rage for two years," said John. "I was either drunk or fighting. It had been the same with other girl friends I'd had. There was something the matter with me."

Cynthia had plenty of opportunities to leave him, but she didn't. She was sure her love would heal his troubled spirit. But John's inner misery ran far deeper than she could touch. "Molly, the cleaning woman, once caught John hitting me, really clouting me," Cynthia admitted. "She said I was a silly girl to get mixed up with someone like that." But Cynthia wasn't about to give up on him. She was totally under his spell. At John's urging, she grew her hair long and dyed it blonde, in honor of Brigitte Bardot.

In August 1959, the Quarry Men were hired to play for the opening night of a new coffeehouse, the Casbah Club. With the help of her two sons, Rory and Pete, Mona Best had turned her large, rambling basement into a club. Word of the opening night spread like wildfire, and teenagers lined up early, snaking from the ground-level entry at the back of the house up the driveway and out the gates. When the doors opened, the crowd impatiently surged forward, eager to pay their admission.

A cheer went up when the Quarry Men launched into their opening number, "Long Tall Sally." The music was raw, wild, exhilarating. People danced, snuck hip-flask liquor into their coffee, and slipped outside to the garden in pairs. Opening night was a wild success, and the Quarry Men were booked for a series of Saturday nights.

Thrilled with his mother's club, seventeen-year-old Pete Best took up drums and put together a house band called the Blackjacks. After years spent beating out rhythm with his hands, or pencils on any flat surface, Pete easily kept a driving rock'n'roll beat on the drums. The Blackjacks hammered out favorites like Little Richard's "Tutti Frutti," Jerry Lee Lewis's "Whole Lot of Shakin' Goin' On," and Carl Perkins's "Honey Don't." The girls went crazy over Pete's quiet, moody good looks.

The Quarry Men, still lacking a drummer and a bass guitar, sometimes asked Pete to sit in with them at the Casbah. And when Stuart won a cash prize for his canvas *Summer Painting*, John talked him into buying a bass instead of art supplies.

Stuart wasn't a natural musician. He fumbled on the guitar, the heavy metal strings of

Paul and John playing the opening night of the Casbah Club on August 29, 1959, watched by John's girlfriend, Cynthia Powell, and her friend.

the bass cutting into his long, thin fingers as he struggled to master the chords. John invited him to perform with them anyway. Paul, already jealous of John spending so much time with Stuart, thought he wasn't good enough to be playing with them. Sometimes he wasn't even in the same key. Paul told Stuart to turn his back on the crowd, so no one would see how badly he was playing.

Now that he was in his third year of art college, Quarry Bank was a distant memory for John. It was time for a new name for the band. John and Paul wanted something like Buddy Holly and the Crickets. The double word play of *cricket*, both a bug and an English sport, cracked them up. They played around with different ideas, and finally inspiration hit. John and Stuart were big fans of Marlon Brando's film, *The Wild One*. In the movie, after Marlon Brando sends Lee Marvin sprawling off his motorcycle, Marvin says to him, "Ever since the club

Marlon Brando on the right, surrounded by his gang in The Wild One, *the movie from which the Beatles took their name.*

split up I've missed you." He pointed to the girls in the gang. "The beetles missed yuh, *all* the beetles missed yuh."

Now they had a name with a clever triple meaning: Not only did it refer to the movie and to an insect, but when they put an *a* in Beatles, the name paid homage to the strong beat driving rock'n'roll. "Fuck me," Paul said later. "It's bikers' molls. . . . We were actually named after girls." For a while they experimented with variations: the Beatals, the Silver Beatles, finally settling on plain Beatles.

In May 1960, they were hired as a backup band for singer Johnny Gentle's eight-day tour of Scotland. They took off in high excitement, jammed into a van. They zigzagged along the coast with their guitars and borrowed amplifiers, ate in cafes, and crammed into cheap hotel rooms at night. The tour was badly organized, and tempers frayed. They bickered and fought with one another, but especially picked on Stuart, who rarely fought back. "We were terrible," John admitted afterwards. "We'd tell him he couldn't sit with us, or eat with us, or tell him to go away, and he did." With their pay barely covering their expenses, they returned to Liverpool broke, hungry, and exhausted.

Their flagging spirits were saved two days later when John talked the owner of the Jacaranda Club, Allan Williams, into letting them play at the club Monday nights when the regular band was off. In exchange for their music, Williams gave them baked beans on toast and as much Coca-Cola as they wanted. Williams soon became an ardent backer of the Beatles and arranged for them to play a weeklong gig when he opened an illegal strip joint in the vice area of the city. The band crowded onto a stage just seven feet square with a spectacularly endowed stripper, Janice, who undulated and peeled off her clothes as they played rock'n'roll. She dropped the last of her clothes with her back to the audience, facing the band. It was almost more than they could stand.

Always on the lookout for another enterprising scheme, Williams heard bands were needed to perform in the clubs in Hamburg, Germany. He arranged a contract for the Beatles and offered to drive them over.

John jumped at the excuse to leave art college. He was through with school for good. There was one snag: The contract called for a five-member band. They needed a drummer. Paul asked Pete Best to audition for them. Pete tried out with his new blue mother-of-pearl drums with real calfskin, playing "Ramrod" and "Shakin' All Over" with John, George, Paul, and Stuart. At the end of twenty minutes they all reached the same conclusion: "Yeh! You're in, Pete!"

They crammed into Williams's minibus with all their instruments and took off for Hamburg on August 16, 1960. In Amsterdam they made a quick stop at a music store to drool over the instruments. John, in a loose black corduroy jacket, pocketed a harmonica. Williams was appalled when John brought it out and bragged to the others. "You're nuts—the lot of you!" He couldn't believe John would jeopardize their whole trip by doing something so risky.

They pulled into Hamburg late the second night and found their way to the Reeperbahn, the main street of the red-light district. Strip joints, dives, and clubs flourished. Sailors

The red-light district where the Beatles performed included clubs like the Mehrer Regina, known to sailors all over the world as the Telephone Bar. Girls sitting at tables each had a phone and a big sign with a number on it. Sailors called the number of the girl they wanted to spend time with.

The Beatles at the Top Ten Club in Hamburg. From left: Paul on piano, Pete Best on drums, Stuart, George, and John.

roamed up and down the sidewalks leering at prostitutes in brightly lit windows, and swaggered into clubs to drink beer. They all seemed to be on the prowl for sex, alcohol, and a good fight.

The Beatles started at the Indra, an old strip club, then moved over to a larger club, the Kaiserkeller. Six nights a week they kept up a grueling schedule, playing forty-five minute sets until two in the morning. They ran through the numbers that excited the crowds in Liverpool: "Tutti Frutti," "Lucille," "Sweet Little Sixteen," and "Johnny B. Goode." The tough, drunk customers and the waiters, hired mostly for their crushing skills as bouncers, frightened even John. Violent fights broke out at the slightest provocation. Then the waiters swung into gear.

Paul and John with an unidentified older man who jumped up onstage in Hamburg and comandeered the microphone.

"The waiters would get their flick knives out, or their truncheons," said John. "And that would be it. I've never seen such killers."

With their insanely long playing hours, the Beatles were forced to come up with new material, working up songs they could improvise and prolong. Their repertoire soon topped over one hundred songs. "What'd I Say," by Ray Charles, became a favorite, with the audience yelling back the lyrics, banging out the rhythm with their beer mugs.

The owner of the club wanted more. *"Mach Schau!"* he yelled at them, "Make show!"

The Beatles jump-started their act into a blistering new level of energy. They leapt on one another's backs, staged mock fights, ate, smoked, and drank onstage. "We used to just be up there frothing at the mouth, foaming, just stomping away," George said. "John used to just dance around like a gorilla and we'd all knock our heads together and things like that." The audience loved it and called them the *"beknakked* Beatles"—the crazy Beatles. Soon they were also nicknamed "*Pilzköpfe*," literally "mushroom heads" because of their English hairstyles.

John went wild. He hurled insults at the crowd, calling them Nazis and Hitlerites. Twisting his body into grotesque shapes, he'd scream at them that they were all "German spassies."

Audience members roared with approval at John's outrageousness, and sent rounds of drinks up to the stage. Soon the Beatles would be as drunk as the customers. The owner of the club kept a sharp eye on them. If they began to flag, he slipped them small pills called prellies. The black-market Preludin sped them up, pushing through the alcohol and fatigue. John thought they were fantastic.

Night after night their music tightened up. They learned to work together intuitively, hitting their notes right on, harmonizing, keeping the rhythm with unerring accuracy. Just a glance or a nod and they'd know what the others were thinking and feeling.

When John wasn't performing, he read the English papers, wrote long letters to Cynthia, drew bizarre cartoons, and walked through town, making fun of disabled people. Unfazed by being in a foreign country, he went shoplifting when the mood hit. The others didn't try to stop him—that was just the way he was. If he thought of it, he'd act on it.

The Beatles bought cheap leather jackets and pants and sharp-pointed boots. They let their hair grow longer, and stopped slicking it back so tightly against the sides. The sailors loved them. So did the local rockers and the Exis—the existentialists from the art colleges who slipped quietly into the clubs to nurse a beer and listen to the music.

One of the Exis, Astrid Kirchherr, fell for Stuart the first night she watched the Beatles perform. As an assistant to a magazine photographer, Astrid quickly saw how interesting they would be to photograph. She was fascinated by them, with their sharp pointed boots, tight pants and jackets. At first, speaking very little English, she was too shy to ask. Finally she got up the courage. When they said yes, she took them to a nearby fairground she thought would make an interesting background. Afterwards she took them home to tea. Her room was painted all black, and lit only with candles. After tea, she drove them back to the Reeperbahn. Her incredible sense of style made her photographs unique, and the Beatles were eager to be photographed again by her.

OVERLEAF: Astrid Kirchherr took the Beatles and their instruments to a fairground near Hamburg for this 1960 shot. From left: Pete, George, John, Paul, and Stuart. Astrid and the other Exis found John menacing and Stuart, who often wore dark glasses even on stage, the most mysterious.

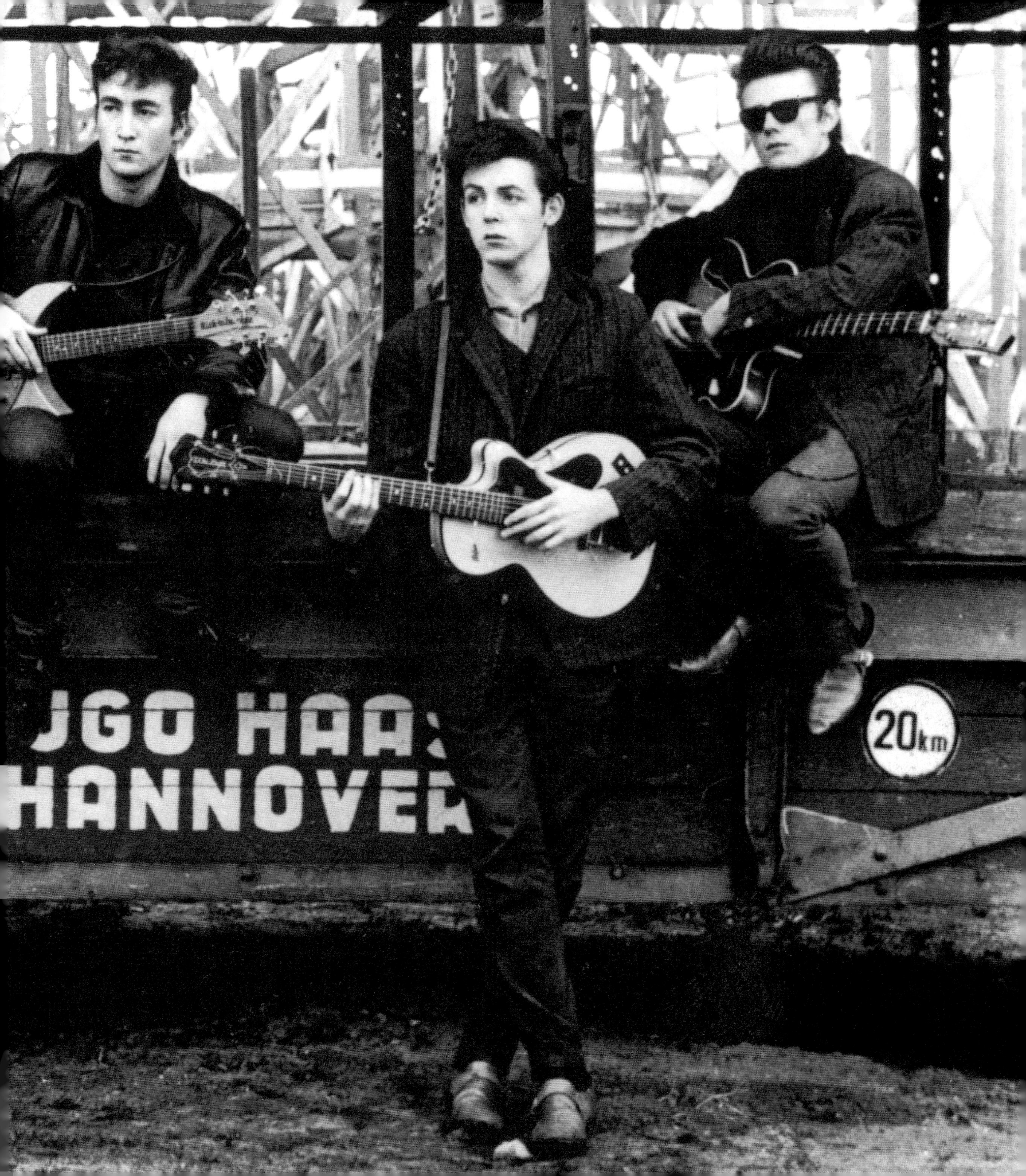
JGO HAA
HANNOVER
20km

Within a few weeks, Stuart began going over alone to Astrid's, and they'd sit side by side on her bed, Astrid with a German-English dictionary, and Stuart with an English-German dictionary. Soon, they were deeply in love. Though he kept performing with the Beatles, it wasn't long before he moved in with her and her mother.

In early December the Beatles decided to switch to the Top Ten, an even better club. The owner of the Kaiserkeller was furious. The authorities suddenly found out that George was only seventeen, underage to be in the clubs after ten P.M. He was ordered to leave the country immediately, and took off, alone and scared on the train. Pete and Paul packed to move to the new club. They defiantly lit a rubber condom in their darkened room to provide light to pack by. It didn't burn long, but was very smoky. The owner accused them of trying to burn the place down and the police marched them off jail for a few hours, then deported them.

With Stuart at Astrid's, John was left alone in Hamburg. He was anxious, afraid to travel by himself, worried sick that someone would realize the amplifier he was carrying on his back hadn't been paid for. He took the long, exhausting train ride back to Liverpool, arriving at Mendips in the middle of the night. He laid low, staying home for nearly two weeks, unsure of what to do next. Even seeing Cynthia didn't lift his spirits.

All four of them were dispirited. At first, the others didn't bother to contact George. He didn't even know they had returned. "I felt ashamed," he said. "After all the big talk when we set off for Hamburg."

Mona Best had them back at the Casbah, and they were booked to play with three other bands at Litherland Town Hall Ballroom in Liverpool on December 27, 1960. They pulled themselves together and opened their Litherland set with Paul screaming out "Long Tall Sally." The song was wild, loud, ecstatic; the Beatles exuded a frenetic, scruffy magnetism. The crowd surged to the front of the room and crushed against the stage. As the Beatles blasted through their Hamburg repertoire, an inexplicable frenzy gripped the teenage audience. "It was that evening," John said, "that we really came out of our shell and let go as we'd played in Hamburg." Beatlemania was born.

Another of Astrid Kirchherr's photos of George, Stuart, and John at the fairground, in front of one of the fair's transport trucks. Astrid's photographs were instrumental in creating the Beatles' early image.

6

BREAKING OUT

1961-1963

"I was a hitter. I couldn't express myself and I hit.
I fought men and I hit women."

STUART SUTCLIFFE RETURNED from Germany in January 1961, just as the Litherland Town Hall booking opened up a floodgate of gigs at local clubs. Some of them were terrifying, as boozed up Teddy boys broke into fights during "Long Tall Sally" and "Hully Gully." Beer bottles, fists, and wooden furniture would fly. Angered by the girls' adoration of the band and their music, the Teds would sometimes wait in the shadows outside afterwards, and try to waylay the group.

At Hambleton Hall in Huyton, George and Paul were both beaten up. On January 30, 1961, after a gig at Lathom Hall, a group of Teds jumped Stuart while he was loading equipment into the van. Alerted by a couple of girls, John and Pete rushed into the melee, punching and kicking as hard as they could. The Teds ran off, but Stuart had already been beaten to the ground and savagely kicked in the head. They got him home, where he collapsed in the doorway, swollen and bruised, blood streaming from a gash in his forehead. It was increasingly clear for Stuart that his interest was not rock'n'roll but art and Astrid.

Stuart and John performing in Hamburg, 1961.

A few days later, the disc jockey at the local Cavern Club, Bob Wooler, booked the Beatles for a lunch set beginning on February 9, 1961. Six weeks later they were given a coveted night booking, where they instantly formed a rapport with their audience. More than five hundred hours of "making show" in Hamburg had turned their performances into a runaway success.

Rockers, shopgirls, young men from nearby offices, students, and factory workers streamed into the Cavern Club on Mathew Street, a filthy, garbage-strewn alley filled with fruit and vegetable warehouses. They squeezed down the steep, uneven steps to the basement with its three narrow rooms, the rough brick walls dripping with moisture. The club was dank and dark. It reeked of cigarette smoke, sweat, and pine disinfectant. The loud music pulsed through the

Fans waiting on the steep steps of the Cavern on Mathew Street to get signed in.

Despite the stifling atmosphere of the Cavern, the Beatles wore their matching black leather outfits to perform.

rooms, bounced off the walls. The audience, crammed in together, clapped and swayed and stamped and screamed. Girls came in their curlers, leaving them in while the other groups played, then rushed to the bathroom to pull them out and back-comb madly before the Beatles performed. The freshly preened girls squeezed together at the front, hoping to be noticed.

John stood behind the mike, knees locked, chin aggressively up, eyes defiant, put-downs and swear words tumbling out of his mouth. He looked like he'd just swung off the back of a motor-cycle. "That John—he was the *animal*," said a Cavern fan. "The girls stood a bit back from him, a bit frightened. You never really knew which way he'd jump." The Beatles' performances left the audience drained, exhausted, and begging for more.

The Beatles ate onstage, joked, and made rude remarks. Pete Best, on drums, rarely joined in, and Stuart only performed occasionally with them. OVERLEAF: *As the Beatles' popularity increased, fans formed long lines on Mathew Street outside the Cavern.*

Their female fans—dubbed the Beatlettes by John—followed them on the streets, giggling, shrieking and pointing, tugging at their clothing, daring each other to grab a quick kiss.

The Beatles' parents weren't nearly as thrilled as the girls. Paul's father, Jim, stopped by occasionally and tried to elbow his way to Paul through the dancing, shrieking, excited fans. "They should have paid you danger money to go down there," he said. "I'd see Paul and the others on the stage, looking like something the cat brought home." Mimi rarely went to the Cavern and was vehement in her criticism. John was almost twenty-one, and had thrown away his chances at art school. Where were all these guitar-playing, pants-splitting gyrations going to get him? She hammered on him to get a decent job.

But John was totally focused on rock'n'roll. He and Paul wanted to make sure they stood out from the other local groups. They searched out the more obscure songs on the B sides of rhythm-and-blues records, like "Anna" by Arthur Alexander, and played them in the Cavern. Boys from other bands wormed their way close to the Beatles and watched their hands intently for interesting riffs and new techniques. The Beatles tentatively tried one of Paul's songs, "Like Dreamers Do." It was a hit with the girls. Encouraged, they added two more of their own, "Hold Me Tight" and "Love Me Do," more complex, bluesier compositions.

At the end of March 1961, the Beatles took off for another three months at the Top Ten Club in Hamburg. Stuart quit the group for good, and they suddenly needed a new bass player. John wasn't about to switch to bass—it was the least sexy instrument in the band. He asked George, who flat-out refused. That left Paul, who got stuck with it.

Toward the end of their booking, they were asked to provide backup for a British singer named Tony Sheridan. On the stage of an empty school auditorium they recorded a few tracks on a portable tape recorder. Sheridan's single, "My Bonnie," was released a few months later and climbed to number five in the German hit parade, but to everyone's intense disappointment, it didn't do a thing in England.

John returned to Liverpool restless and unhappy. He sent long letters back to Stuart, full of his dark, depressed thoughts. "I remember a time when everyone I loved hated me because I hated them so what so what so fucking what. . . . I can't remember anything without a sadness so deep that it hardly becomes known to me." Stuart's long, heartfelt

Astrid and Stuart in Hamburg. A teacher at the Staatliche Hochschule für Bildende Künste (State Institute of Art Instruction), impressed with Stuart's talent, arranged for him to receive a grant.

return letters were full of Astrid and his artwork. He also complained of blinding headaches and seizures, perhaps caused by the horrific beating he'd received outside Lathom Hall.

For his twenty-first birthday in October, John received a generous check from his aunt in Scotland. He and Paul immediately took off on a two-week trip to Paris, lounging around Left Bank cafes and taking in the local rock scene. They restyled their hair, easing up on the grease, and letting the front fall across their foreheads in the popular "French" cut being worn in France and Germany. When John's money ran out, they returned to Liverpool and their waiting gigs.

A few weeks later, a young man in a leather jacket, named Raymond Jones, walked into the biggest record store in Liverpool, NEMS, and asked if they had a copy of "My Bonnie." The manager of the store, Brian Epstein, had never heard of it, but prided himself on locating any record a customer wanted. Several others came into the store, eagerly asking for the same record. Brian was mystified—who were these Beatles?

He discovered they were playing a few blocks away at the Cavern. On November 9, briefcase in hand, he crept trepidatiously down the steep stairs of the club to see what all the excitement was about.

In his pin-striped business suit and tie, Brian stood at the back of the crowd, hands immaculate, shoes polished, hair cut short. The Beatles in their scruffy black leather jackets played wild, seductive rock'n'roll songs, talking, eating, and shouting at the audience. Brian was captivated.

Only twenty-seven years old, Brian was in charge of nine record stores in the family business. Raised by a nanny in a wealthy Jewish family in Liverpool, he'd bounced through several private schools and briefly tried a career in acting before settling down in his family's record stores.

Brian returned again and again to the Cavern to watch the Beatles. In December 1961, he invited them to his office and offered to be their manager. The Beatles were impressed. He was a well-dressed, well-spoken businessman without a trace of a Scouse accent. He even had his own car, a beautiful new Ford Zodiac. For a few moments no one spoke, then John broke the silence with a gruff yes. It was settled. Brian would manage them.

The first thing Brian did was clean up their image. He talked them out of their worn leather jackets and into matching suits. He had them work out a strict program, playing their best numbers, and forbade them from eating, drinking, and heckling audience members during their performances. With his theatrical flair, Brian insisted they all learn to bow together from the waist, dramatically holding the deep bow for several seconds. John resented cleaning up, but he wanted the band to make it big. It was worth doing what Brian said.

Brian talked the head of Decca Records into giving them an audition for a record contract, and on a bitterly cold, snowy New Year's Day, 1962, the Beatles nervously trouped into a real London studio for the first time. Their battered old equipment appalled the engineer, who

As soon as Brian Epstein became the Beatles' manager, he began taking meticulous notes about exactly what he expected from them. He was particularly annoyed by their habit of arriving late for gigs, and insisted they arrive punctually.

insisted they use the unfamiliar studio amplifiers. They whipped through fifteen songs, three of them their own compositions. Listening to the playbacks, the Beatles thought they sounded fantastic. Even the engineer was excited, and promised to let them know Decca's answer soon. Everyone went home in high spirits, convinced they were on their way to stardom.

The excitement carried over to Liverpool, and the Cavern DJ, Bob Wooler, added a new spin to their introduction, lavishly calling them "recording stars." But the weeks dragged by with no news as Brian tried repeatedly to get a response from Decca. Finally in March, Decca turned them down. Groups with guitars, they said, were on their way out.

On April 11, 1962, the Beatles flew back to Hamburg for a booking in one of the newest of the Reeperbahn clubs, the Star-Club. Astrid was waiting for them at the airport with terrible news: Stuart had died the day before of a brain hemorrhage as an ambulance rushed him to the hospital.

John didn't cry. "He went into this hysterical laugher," said Astrid, "and couldn't stop." Two days later the Beatles opened at the Star-Club, "making show," desperately acting as if nothing had happened.

John, painfully familiar with losing people he loved, was determined to push forward, but

Astrid fell into a profound depression. John refused to let her flounder. "Make up your mind," he said roughly to her. "You either live or die. You can't be in the middle." He insisted she come to the club and watch them play, rather than stay at home, shut up in her room. It was tough advice, but it worked.

While they were gone, Brian threw himself into making the rounds of recording companies. But no one was remotely interested in taking on a rock'n'roll band from Liverpool. Brian set himself an ultimatum: He'd take one more trip to London and give himself twenty-four hours to hustle up an audition before he threw in the towel.

He finally struck pay dirt. George Martin, a producer at EMI studios, said he was willing to audition the Beatles, but no promises. The Beatles flew back from Hamburg and on June 6 headed into the London studio at 3 Abbey Road for an audition. John was thrilled when Martin revealed he produced records by Goon members Peter Sellers and Spike Milligan.

Martin was impressed by the Beatles, but not by their music. As a classically trained oboist, he wasn't wild about their rough-textured rock'n'roll. But he found them highly charismatic, and realized that if he liked being with them, the audience would feel the same way. After running through a number of songs, they were given the thumbs-up to record four: "Besame Mucho" and three by Lennon-McCartney, "Love Me Do," "P. S. I Love You," and "Ask Me Why."

The Cavern threw a "Welcome Home" night and the Beatles shattered all previous attendance records. Brian booked them on a grueling schedule: Between June 6 and July 31 they played sixty-two live performances, including invaluable out-of-town dates as Brian widened their territory.

But just as things were blowing wide open, one Saturday morning Cynthia tearfully blurted out shocking news to John: She was pregnant. She watched, her heart pounding in her chest, as he looked at her, speechless, his eyes panic-stricken. But John knew there was only one thing to do: A few weeks later, on August 23, 1962, John and Cynthia were quickly married at the Mount Pleasant Register Office with Brian, Paul, and George attending. Mimi, furious they'd gotten themselves into trouble, refused to come.

Only twenty-one, John was embarrassed to be a married man. "It was like walking about with odd socks on, your fly open." Brian, afraid the fans would be upset, asked Cynthia and John to keep their marriage a secret.

There was one more big change in August. For some time the Beatles had been feeling that Pete's drumming just wasn't good enough. At the June 6 EMI audition, George Martin had pulled Brian aside and told him Pete's drumming wasn't what he wanted. If they did make a record, he'd hire a session drummer. It was the last straw. Behind Pete's back, John, Paul, and George decided on another drummer. They had Brian call Pete into his office and tell him they wanted him out. "We were cowards when we sacked him," John said. "We made Brian do it."

Pete, suddenly thrown out with no warning, was devastated. When news leaked out, some of the Cavern fans were furious. With his handsome, moody good looks, Pete was their favorite. In a scuffle outside the club with angry fans, George was punched in the eye.

Another Liverpool drummer the Beatles knew from Hamburg, Ringo Starr, replaced Pete. They'd played alternating sets with his band, Rory Storm and the Hurricanes, at the Kaiserkeller and when Pete had missed several performances at the Cavern, Ringo sat in with them. Not only could Ringo keep a steady rock'n'roll beat, he had a way of getting something *more* out of his drums, an indefinable, unique sound only he could produce.

Born on July 7, 1940, in the rough, working-class area of Dingle, Ringo was christened Richard Starkey, after his father. Ringo's parents separated when he was three, and his mother went back to work as a waitress. At six, Ringo's appendix burst. Complications from his emergency appendectomy kept him in the hospital for more than a year.

Ringo went back to school unable to read or

Ringo didn't understand why the Beatles would replace sexy Pete Best with him. Though he had a great sense of style, he didn't consider himself good looking. The hair on his right temple turned gray when he was young, perhaps due to illness.

write, but amazingly cheerful and easygoing. He managed to scrape along in school, but at thirteen he developed a problem with his lungs and was put in a children's sanatorium for the next two years. When he finally got out, he was hopelessly behind academically. At fifteen, he was just old enough to legally quit school, and he refused to go back. His mother was terribly worried about what kind of work he'd be able to do. The long hospitalizations had left him small, thin, and weak. He wasn't strong enough to work on the docks and had no proper schooling for any kind of office job.

Ringo cycled through several dead-end jobs, then found work as an apprentice pipe fitter. When the skiffle craze hit, he joined an impromptu in-house band as the drummer, playing for the other apprentices at lunchtime. He turned out to have a knack for drumming and by late 1959 was playing with the Hurricanes.

ABOVE: Ringo (far right) with his group Rory Storm and the Hurricanes. Because of the big, chunky rings he wore, Rory encouraged him to change his name from Richard to Ringo and shorten his last name to Starr. RIGHT: The Beatles in the studio the first time they recorded with Ringo.

When the Hurricanes went through a low spell with few bookings, Ringo decided to emigrate to the United States. He read that American bluesman Lightnin' Hopkins came from Houston, Texas, and he applied to the U.S. Consul to move to Houston. "Then the really big forms arrived," Ringo said. "All about was your grandfather's Great Dane a Commie. I couldn't understand them. If I had, I would definitely have gone."

With Pete out and Ringo in, George Martin called them back to London to record on September 4, 1962. They were still nervous in the studio, and refused to put on headphones. When John launched into "Love Me Do," Martin realized the song would be immeasurably strengthened by John's haunting, bluesy harmonica playing. Martin had Paul take the lead, his voice quavering as he sang it for the first time.

Martin also had found a song for them he was sure would be a huge hit, "How Do You Do It." Paul and John's confidence had grown, and they resented being asked to record a song *anybody* could do. They told Martin they wanted to record their own compositions. Martin went through the roof. He was sure he knew what would be a hit better than they did. Grudgingly, they recorded the song for him.

On September 11, they returned to the studio to record four more songs they'd written, including "Please Please Me." John had written it at Mendips, intrigued by making double use of the word "please." The recording went beautifully, John's voice sexy and insistent, insinuating more than the lyrics spelled out.

When they finished, Martin pressed the intercom button in the control room and said, "Gentlemen, you've just made your first number-one record." Martin was right. The song shot up the charts to number one.

In an exhausting ten-hour session on February 11, 1963, the Beatles recorded ten more songs for their first album, *Please Please Me*. Martin saved for last their popular, driving song "Twist and Shout." John, screaming out the lead, made a sound in his throat like tearing flesh. It had to be right the first time.

By the time "She Loves You" hit number one in August 1963, the Beatles were in demand for bookings on radio and television shows all over England. Frantic, hysterical fans would swarm around stage doors and shove into the dressing room. Neil Aspinall, an old school friend who drove them to their gigs and set up their equipment, was overwhelmed. Every night he had a new road to drive, new stagehands to deal with, and constant, crushing masses of fans to get the Beatles through. Brian asked Mal Evans, a big, strong, easygoing bouncer from the Cavern, to join them on the road.

On April 8, 1963, while John was on tour, Cynthia gave birth to a son, Julian, named in honor of John's mother. Cynthia was panic-stricken when she discovered Julian had a prominent mole on his head. With John's horror of physical deformities, how would he react when he found his child wasn't perfect?

John rushed home a few days later and peppered her with questions: How had the birth been, what was the baby like? Cynthia decided not to hide Julian's mole from John. "Oh he's beautiful, wonderful, John," she said, "but he has this birth mark on his head."

Paul and John each usually had a microphone, and George would share with one of them. In this 1963 Cavern photograph, George sings with John. Because of Paul's left-handed guitar playing, it was awkward for anyone to stand to his right side.

It didn't seem to bother John. He held Julian in his arms, crooning, "Who's going to be a famous little rocker like his dad then?"

As soon as he'd seen his new baby, John took off with Brian on a vacation to Spain. Cynthia swallowed her disappointment, rationalizing that John had been working hard recording and touring and needed some time to unwind.

John wanted to get to know Brian better. He introduced Brian to pills, partly to get him to open up and talk about himself. There was also something titillating about the vacation: Brian had admitted to John that he was gay, with the warning, "Don't ever throw it back in me face that I'm a fag." They sat together in the cafes, John asking

Brian to tell him which boys he liked as they walked by. John played a new song he was working on, "Bad to Me," for Brian. "It was almost a love affair, but not quite," John said later. "It was never consummated."

Shortly after they got home, Paul celebrated his twenty-first birthday with a huge, rowdy outdoor party. The music was loud, the alcohol flowed freely. Rumors swirled around that John was involved with Brian. Cavern DJ Bob Wooler made a snide crack to John about his "Spanish honeymoon."

In a drunken fury, John attacked Wooler, injuring him so badly, Wooler had to be rushed to the hospital. "I smashed him up," John said. "I broke his bloody ribs for him." Afterwards he sat cradling his head in his hands, moaning over and over again, "What have I done?"

Wooler spent several weeks recovering. Not only physically hurt, he was profoundly upset that John had turned on him so violently. He'd been a loyal admirer, promoter, and friend. Brian smoothed things over, arranging a cash settlement and insisting John formally apologize.

Brian had a London tailor make matching suits for the Beatles of gray wool and mohair. Brian insisted they wear the suits with heavily starched white shirts, ties, and cuff links in the broad cuffs.

7

BEATLEMANIA

1963-1965

*"It was like being in the eye of a hurricane. You'd wake up
in a concert and think, Wow, how did I get here?"*

ON SUNDAY, SEPTEMBER 15th, 1963 the Beatles played at the Royal Albert Hall in London. Shepherded outside for a photo session, they stood on a set of wide stairs, barely able to keep up with the incredible changes they were going through. "We looked at each other," Paul said, "and we were thinking, this is it! London! The Albert Hall! We felt like gods! We felt like fucking gods!"

In October the Beatles were invited to play at the Royal Command Variety Performance, a glittering, snobbish event attended by the British royal family. An uproar broke out in the newspapers that had begun reporting on their activities. The Beatles were accused of selling out, playing for the Establishment. John agreed—the point of rock'n'roll was to rebel against upper-class values. Ringo, with his sweet, forthright personality, diffused the controversy, saying, "I just want to play me drums for the Queen Mum."

The Beatles look over a script at Abbey Road Studio in London, 1964.

Prominent, wealthy members of society in their best evening clothes filled the Prince of Wales Theater on November 4. Members of the royal family sat in their box, watching and politely clapping. After rocking through three numbers, John introduced "Twist and Shout," their final number. "Will the people in the cheaper seats clap your hands?" he asked devilishly. "And the rest of you, if you'll just rattle your jewelry."

Watching from a seat in the audience, Brian was horrified. After a shocked moment of silence, the audience roared with laugher. The Beatles tore through "Twist and Shout," bowed to the audience, then to the royal box, and sprinted off the stage.

With London the center of the music world, it was obvious the Beatles needed to move. Brian was the first to leave Liverpool, quickly followed by the four Beatles. Cynthia was delighted when she and John found an apartment off Cromwell Road in London, and relieved when word got out he was married and had a baby son. She no longer needed to hide.

Cynthia with baby Julian and groceries in his pram.

But John's fame caused a huge problem. Crowds of fans, almost all young women, gathered outside the apartment armed with sleeping bags and thermoses full of hot tea, determined to wait for their new idol to come home. They'd stuff chewing gum in the lock to delay John once he arrived, then, shrieking and crying, they'd pull on his clothes, tug at his hair, beg for autographs.

Getting all four Beatles through the crowds now gathering at train stations, airports, and concert halls required a choreographed strategy: They intentionally arrived late and blitzed through the crowd at a dead run. Once onstage, they couldn't hear their own voices or instruments over the screaming fans. Offstage, they were forced to stay cooped up in hotel rooms and dingy backstage dressing rooms. John, asked what a weeklong fall tour of Sweden had been like, replied, "A room and a car and a car and a room."

To while away the long hours on the road, John read voraciously from books and newspapers. He soaked up ideas from articles and fragments of overheard conversations, and wrote stories and nonsensical verses.

John and Paul dropped into songwriting mode anywhere they were: in hotel rooms, the car, even in the dressing room as they waited to go onstage. All they needed was an idea, perhaps a line or two, and a piano or guitar. They'd toss lyrics and musical riffs back and forth and come up with a couple of verses and a chorus. "Lyrics didn't really count," John said, "as long as we had some vague theme: 'She loves you, he loves her, and they love each other.' It was the hook and the line and the sound we were going for." While many songwriters would work on a song for weeks or even months, John and Paul usually had a song in a couple of hours.

BELOW and OVERLEAF: August 1963, Paul and John during a break in filming a television show in Birmingham, England.

Paul with his girlfriend, Jane Asher, 1963.

In London, Paul moved in with Jane Asher, a talented redheaded actress, and her parents. Paul was fascinated by the whole family and their involvement in classical music and theater. He and Jane immediately hit the newspapers as fashionable London flooded them with invitations for theatrical openings and trendy parties.

Though they could write anywhere, Paul and John discovered the quiet music room in the Ashers' basement was ideal. One day they sat together at the piano in the music room, fiddling with different chords, seeing what they could come up with. They had just a few words—"Oh you-u . . . got that something . . ."—when Paul hit a new chord. "That's *it*!" John said. "Do that again!" In no time, they had "I Want to Hold Your Hand."

In their songwriting, Paul often came up with tender, sweet lyrics about love, while John moaned about how bad the world was treating him. Paul could be melodic, with a love of ballads, while John could be edgy, fast, and dark. It was a perfect balance. "He provided a lightness, an optimism," John said, "while I would always go for the sadness, the discords, a certain bluesy edge."

The latest new Motown, rhythm-and-blues, or rock'n'roll song fired them up. "We used to steal consciously," Paul explained, "particularly from American black acts like the Marvelettes and alter it a bit. Something you love, something you're passionate about, is always a great starting point."

Their second album, *With the Beatles*, was released on November 22, 1963, the same day President John F. Kennedy was assassinated in Dallas, Texas. Within a week, sales topped more than half a million copies, and the band was trotted out for a renewed round of press conferences. They used a sharp-edged humor to alleviate their irritation when asked inane questions.

The Beatles in the pressroom at JFK International Airport just after their arrival on February 7, 1964.

A reporter discovered someone at Decca had turned the band down. "He must be kicking himself now," the journalist said.

"I 'ope he kicks himself to death," one of the Beatles replied.

"Are those wigs you're wearing?" a reporter asked.

"If they are," John replied, "they must be the only wigs with dandruff."

"I Want to Hold Your Hand," released as a single at the end of the 1963 in both Britain and America, shot to the top of both countries' charts. It was their first song to make it big in America. With a tour of the United States already in the planning stages, Brian went into over-drive with a crash publicity program. Five million posters were plastered up in towns across America announcing the Beatles' imminent arrival. Radio stations, which were mailed free copies of all the Beatles previous English hits, spun their records nonstop. *Life* magazine ran a lavishly photographed article, and free T-shirts were promised to anyone who met the Beatles at the newly named John F. Kennedy International airport in New York. Word spread like wildfire: The Beatles would appear live on *The Ed Sullivan Show* on February ninth.

Exiting the plane after a long transatlantic flight, the Beatles were shocked to find three thousand screaming, hysterical fans waiting for them at the airport. Hustled through the crowd

The Beatles making their American debut on The Ed Sullivan Show on February 9, 1964. During their performance of "Till There Was You," each of their first names were superimposed on the screen. John's had the additional caption, "Sorry Girls, He's Married."

Fans at The Ed Sullivan Show.

for a press conference, they faced reporters jammed in elbow to elbow, eager for copy to take back to their newspapers. The Beatles didn't understand their huge welcome. America was home to a constellation of incredible musicians: the bluesmen who'd inspired them, Elvis with his sultry voice and Hollywood films, the Beach Boys and their sun-and-surf harmonies of California, Bob Dylan and his cutting protest songs—it was all happening here in America.

They didn't realize the tremendous pall that hung over America since Kennedy's assassination. America needed something new, a lightness and hope that things could look up again. A palpable, contagious excitement gripped the audience as the Beatles played five songs on *The Ed Sullivan Show*. In the beginning of the show, they did "All My Loving," "Till There Was You," and "She Loves You." In the second half they did two more: "I Saw Her Standing There" and "I Want to Hold Your Hand." More than seventy-three million viewers tuned in, making it the most-watched television show ever.

Then they were off by train to Washington, D.C., where the Beatles played their first American concert, for a crowd of more than eight thousand at the Washington Coliseum.

THE SHOREHAM—WASHINGTON, D.C.
1. Beethoven
2. From me to you
3. I saw her standing there
4. This Boy
5. All my loving
6. I wanna be your man
7. Please Please Me
8. Till there was you
9. She loves you
10. I want to hold your hand
11. Twist and Shout
12. Long Tall Sally

On February 11, 1964, the Beatles played the Coliseum in Washington, D.C. John wrote out the set list (left) and Paul put it on top of one of the two Vox amplifiers. The smudges are a mixture of sweat and the makeup they wore under the bright stage lights.

Fans screamed and swooned and cried and screamed some more. The next day, pandemonium greeted their two shows at Carnegie Hall in New York City, where more than three hundred policeman were hired to insure the Beatles' safety. Whisked away afterwards to Florida, the Beatles were secreted in a borrowed home belonging to a millionaire. Convertibles, yachts, and swimming pools were at their disposal. Gorgeous, tanned women in bikinis were everywhere.

Overnight they'd stepped right into the middle of the sun-drenched American dream they'd seen on television as kids: palm trees and rolling surf, fast cars, fast money, and notoriety. They had hoped, longed, to make it big in America. But they had thought they'd have to work for it—they never imagined it would come rushing at them like this. It was amazing and inexplicable. America had surrendered to the Beatles.

Their schedule was far too packed for them to sit around crowing about their accomplishments. They needed to get back to London. There were songs to write; albums to record; concerts, radio, and television appearances lined up; and a movie to film.

On March 2, 1964, they jumped into shooting a black-and-white feature film. *A Hard Day's Night* was a dizzying, kaleidoscopic, cinema-verité look at the Beatles on tour, running from venue to venue, chased by fans, performing new songs.

John liked the film, feeling it was a genuine look at their manic touring life. For George, there was a special bonus: One of the extras in the film, nineteen-year old model Patti Boyd, caught his eye. It wasn't long before they were seen together around London.

While all four Beatles were considered quick-witted, John established himself as the "literary Beatle" in late March with the release of his first book, *In His Own Write*. Full of John's ironic, raw humor in short stories, musings, poems, and bizarre ink sketches, it sold out its first printing of one hundred thousand in one day. Critics fell all over themselves praising *In His Own Write*, except for a pious few who lamented the death of the English language. John, never able to master spelling, claimed he'd developed his short, quirky writing style to cover up dyslexia. Publishing a book was deeply satisfying—writing gave him a creative outlet he didn't feel he had in his songs.

After a few hurried appearances to promote his book, John took off with the other Beatles on tours of Europe, Hong Kong, Australia, and New Zealand. Beatlemania kept going ballistic: In Adelaide, Australia, three hundred thousand fans greeted the Beatles.

George signs autographs for fans at a railroad station in London during filming of A Hard Day's Night.

With fame came money. In July 1964, John and Cynthia bought a twenty-seven room mansion in the "stockbroker belt" just south of London. John hired a staff and put in a swimming pool. Up in the attic he set up a music room with two pianos, tape decks, and guitars. Downstairs he had a favorite sofa tucked into a small room off the kitchen, where he read the paper, watched television, and jotted down ideas and drawings.

June, 1964: 300,000 fans turned out to greet the Beatles on their Australian tour. The crowds reminded many of a Hitler Youth rally, and John and Paul gave a Nazi-style salute during one of their balcony appearances. Fortunately for the Beatles, the resulting controversy quickly died down.

John had little time to unwind in his new house, as the Beatles left Britain on August 18 for another American tour. Bob Dylan came to visit in their New York City hotel room. They offered him wine. He pulled out a baggie of marijuana, rolled a joint, and passed it around. None of the Beatles had ever smoked pot. When it was gone, he rolled another. Paul looked over at impeccably dressed, perfectly mannered Brian smoking the stubby end of a joint, and broke into giggles—he thought Brian looked like a "tramp smoking a dog-end," which none of them had done since they were dirt poor. They spent the evening smoking and drinking, laughing hilariously, proud to have been turned on for the first time by Dylan, initiated by the great folk master of them all.

Far more important to John was the influence Dylan had on his songwriting. John thought the overall feel of the music was what was important; for Dylan, it was the words. "Blowin' in the Wind" and his other songs tackled political and personal

Bob Dylan at Columbia Records in New York 1963-64.

issues straight-on. Even his love songs like "Girl from the North Country" were poignant and intense. Talking to Dylan and listening to his records, John got it: The words to a song could convey something important to him, just as his other writings did.

The Beatles blasted their way through twenty-five American cities, doing shows in huge baseball stadiums, convention halls, and amphitheaters, playing music they couldn't hear, performing in cities they never saw, except for brief flashes of crowded streets from the windows of their speeding car.

OVERLEAF: The Beatles' September 11, 1964, concert at the Gator Bowl in Jacksonville, Florida, was nearly canceled. Hurricane Dora had just roared through, leaving a disaster area. Winds still gusted to forty miles an hour, and Ringo's drums had to be nailed to the stage to keep them from blowing away.

Before each show, their dressing room filled up with police, reporters, and local promoters. The hysteria surrounding the Beatles was so contagious that disabled children and adults showed up, hoping the Beatles had magical curative powers, and were allowed past the local security men. John hated having them in the crowded room. Finally John or one of the others would yell at their road manager, Neil Aspinall, "Cripples, Neil," and Mal Evans would clear the room. It became a secret shorthand: When someone dubious approached, or something weird was in the air, someone would shout, "Cripples!" to put the others on alert.

An outrageous, no-restraints party scene broke the dreary boredom and claustrophobia of their hotel rooms. Booze, pills, and joints were consumed in astonishing amounts. After the show, the vigilant, helpful roadies, Mal and Neil, would pull four good-looking girls past the police lines to meet the Beatles. "Of course there were orgies!" Neil said. "There was an orgy in every town. It's only a miracle the press didn't get a hold of it." Members of the press who were present *did* know all about it, but nobody wanted to blow the whistle on the Beatles. There was more than enough to smoke and drink for everyone.

While the press and hangers-on were having the time of their lives, Brian's life was a whirlwind of planning, managing, and strategizing as he looked after every detail of the Beatles' well-being. He oversaw their contracts, organized press conferences and tours, kept them fully scheduled. The stress of taking the Beatles from provincial Liverpool lads to world-wide stars ate away at him. He could be unfailingly polite one moment, then throw a peevish temper tantrum the next. He began to take pills for insomnia at night and nerves during the day. John teased him mercilessly. Nothing was off-limits to John's scathing tongue. When Brian asked for title ideas for the autobiography he was writing, John suggested "Queer Jew." Brian took whatever John dished out, and stayed steadfastly loyal to him and the rest of the Beatles. They weren't just a job to him: They were a calling.

John hated what they had become. "It's like we're four freaks being wheeled out to be seen, shake our hair about, and get back in our cage afterwards," he complained. It didn't matter what they sang, since no one could hear them over all the screaming. "Beatles concerts are nothing to do with music any more," he said cynically. "They're just bloody tribal rites." The others were more tolerant. If this was what it took to be successful, they'd do it. John went along, but his resentment was building, fueling sharp retorts, belligerent moods, and screamed obscenities from stage, which the audience couldn't hear over their own shrieking.

In June 1965, the Beatles played in three cities in Italy as part of a short two-week European tour. In Rome, an enthusiastic fan managed to get up onstage and make a grab for John's hat.

The Beatles returned from their American tour exhausted. They'd played thirty-one shows in twenty-five cities, smiled cheerily for hundreds of publicity shots, made clever quips at untold numbers of radio, press, and television interviews, and traveled more than twenty-two thousand miles, all in just thirty-three days. John crumpled onto his favorite couch in his twenty-seven-room mansion, worn out and agitated, his temper explosive. "He'd just come home from a tour, all hyped up and nervous, and somebody was going to get it," Cynthia said. "It was unfair that Julian and I were the people he chose." John would blow his top, then ashamed, he'd apologize and be sweet and understanding. Cynthia decided the best thing for her marriage was to remain herself, a steady person John could come home to. Paul, knowing John, thought Cynthia was making a hopeless attempt to domesticate him.

Paul, George, and Ringo followed John's lead and bought mansions, and spent small fortunes having them fixed up. In the evenings they went out on the town, welcome every-where in the swinging nightclub scene as they moved restlessly from club to club, drinking, dancing, and picking up women for one-night stands. Even Paul had a measure of freedom—after all, he and Jane weren't married. The newly available birth control pill eradicated the danger of pregnancy, and gonorrhea and syphilis could be knocked out with powerful antibiotics. The Beatles and London roared into the Swinging Sixties together.

People let their hair grow long and wore it loose. Drab suits were cast aside for paisley shirts, striped pants, and bold, colorful ties. A young London designer, Mary Quant, popularized miniskirts. King's Road and Carnaby Street filled with clothing boutiques jammed full of exuberant, revealing clothes, and whimsical accessories. "Before the pill there couldn't really be a true emancipation," Mary Quant explained. It was as if now women could say, "Wow—look at me!—Isn't it lovely? At last, at last!" Pop and op art were in.

With the social fabric of Britain shaking loose, the Beatles played up their Scouse accents and made the most of their Liverpool roots. John, asked if he was confused by which silverware to use, snapped back that it wasn't a problem: He ate with his hands.

Jealous of the unmarried Beatles' freedom, John carried on continuous affairs, hiding them from Cynthia. He'd creep home well past midnight and sleep in till early afternoon while Cynthia kept Julian from bothering him. When he woke up, she brought him breakfast and tea in bed. John would bury himself in the newspaper or stare vacantly at the television. He often found it hard to connect with Cynthia and Julian. His refuge was his music room. Undisturbed, he could get stoned, write songs, play his guitar, and dream.

The Beatles began filming a second movie, *Help!*, in February 1965. This time the film was shot in color, and the script was set in the Bahamas and the Austrian Alps, with the Beatles being chased by a cult who wanted to sacrifice Ringo to get his ring. For most of the shooting, the Beatles were all stoned out of their minds. It didn't seem to bother anyone.

In May, toward the end of shooting the film, Paul woke up with a melody running through his head. He went straight from his bed to the piano, using the words "scrambled eggs" as a place holder while he played with the chords. Recorded in June, "Yesterday," was included on the *Help!* album. Dylan's musical inspiration showed up in John's title song, a rowdy, rock'n'roll tune with personal, revealing lyrics. "I was fat and depressed and I *was* crying out for help," John said.

Returning home one day, John was met at the house by an uncomfortable Cynthia and a surprise guest: his father. Working only a few miles away as a dishwasher, Freddie had turned

March 1965: John and Paul during the filming of Help!

up looking to reestablish his relationship with his long-lost son. John hadn't seen his father since he was five years old. Freddie went into detail about what a hard life he'd had, and it was clear he was after money. John was terribly embarrassed. "He was in and out of the room like a cat on a hot tin roof," Cynthia said.

Knowing he was on to a good thing, Freddie sold his life story to *Tit Bits* magazine, recorded his own pop record, and married Pauline Jones, a nineteen-year-old Beatles fan. John grudgingly bought them a house and gave them a monthly stipend. When Freddie kept dropping by, wanting more, John finally slammed the door in his father's face.

John saw Mimi when he could, and often talked with her on the phone. The mayhem of Beatlemania was washing over her as well. Fans got hold of her phone number no matter how often she changed it. They came to Liverpool and camped out on her front lawn, singing, shrieking, giggling, and talking under her windows all night long. If she left the

John with his aunt Mimi, 1965.

back door unlocked, they'd creep in and steal cups, silverware—anything they thought had been touched by John. Painfully aware of her distress, John finally insisted she move, and bought her a beautiful house in the seaside town of Bournemouth, overlooking the harbor. With Mimi no longer at John's childhood home, the fans' pilgrimages dwindled.

In the summer of 1965, John's second book, *A Spaniard in the Works*, came out, full of more of his parodies, cartoons, and puns. The Beatles dashed off on another sold-out concert tour of the United States. John's moods were volatile. He wrote Cynthia: "I don't know what's the matter with me—It's not the tour that's so different from other tours—I mean I'm having lots of laughs (you know the type he! he!) but in between the laughs there is such a drop—I mean there seems no in between feelings."

During the madness of touring, the Beatles' main support came from one another. "When we actually got in that limo," Paul said, "that was the real thing. That was where we drew our strength from. We were able to withdraw into this private world of our own."

George Martin noticed the same thing. As close as he was to the Beatles, he was not part of that private world. "It was like a fort, really, with four corners, that was impregnable," Martin explained. "Nobody got inside that fort once they were together, not even Brian Epstein, nor I. . . . They had an empathy and a kind of mind-reading business, an almost kinetic energy, such that when they were together they seemed to become another dimension."

Musically, they intuitively tuned in to one another, effortlessly getting in sync the moment they began playing. Paul was the best all-round musician, great on the bass, drums, or piano. George could give any rock'n'roll guitarist a run for his money. John wasn't technically very good, but as he put it, he could make the guitar "fucking howl and move." With Ringo on drums and George Martin in the studio, it wasn't a question of *if* a release would hit number one—it was just a question of how fast.

April 1964: The Beatles being driven to the Norfolk Airport for a private flight to Scotland, where they did three shows in two nights in Edinburgh and Glasgow, taping radio and television interviews before the performances.

With no formal musical training, the Beatles were utterly ignorant of the rigid rules governing music. Instead, they wrote by ear and untrained instinct, going for chord progressions that appealed to them. George Martin listened with a growing respect. The Beatles had freedom to think in ways he wouldn't even have dreamed of. It made for unique, powerful music.

"They were doing things nobody was doing," Bob Dylan noticed as he watched their hits fly into the American Top Ten. "Their chords were outrageous, just outrageous, and their harmonies made it all valid. . . . But I kept it to myself that I really dug them. . . . Everybody else thought they were for the teenyboppers, that they were gonna pass right away. But it was obvious to me that they had staying power. I knew they were pointing the direction that music had to go."

8

TRAPPED

1965-1967

"I've always needed a drug to survive. The others too, but I always had more, I always took more pills and more of everything, cause I'm more crazy."

THE BEATLES' IMAGE changed radically on October 26, 1965, when the queen awarded them the prestigious title of Members of the Order of the British Empire, the first time any rock'n'rollers had been honored with an MBE. John's first impulse was to turn down the award, but Brian said it was unthinkable to refuse the queen. John reluctantly participated in the sober, ritual-bound ceremony after ducking into the bathroom to get stoned.

But he felt like he'd sold out, a feeling he was having with increasing frequency. "It just happens bit by bit, until this complete craziness surrounds you," said John, "and you're doing exactly what you don't want to do with people you can't stand—the people you hated when you were ten." At Christmastime, John took the medal down to Mimi in her new home and told her to keep it. Bursting with pride, she gave it a place of honor on top of her television set.

In October 1965, the Beatles headed into the studio to record *Rubber Soul*. It was their sixth British album, following *Help!* (August 1965), *Beatles for Sale* (December 1964), *A Hard Day's Night* (July 1964), *With the Beatles* (November 1963), and *Please Please Me* (March 1963).

John photographed in a fish-eye lens while on location shooting How I Won the War.

In America, their albums were marketed under different titles, the songs often repackaged, making *Rubber Soul* their eleventh release.

In the Abbey Road studio, four-track recording had replaced two-track. The miraculous new technology gave the Beatles a chance to record instrumental, vocal, and rhythm tracks individually, erasing and rerecording tracks to get exactly what they wanted. Instead of whipping manically through their recording in ten hours as they had done with their first album, *Please Please Me*, they put in long hours at the studio for two weeks, laying down exactly what they wanted on each track.

George Martin listened soberly to George's lead guitar parts, and if he didn't like what he heard, he'd demonstrate what he wanted on the piano. Like John and Paul, he dominated George's contributions. "I was," Martin said, "always rather beastly to George." Caught up in their own work, John and Paul dismissed the amazing work George was doing. On *Rubber Soul*, they grudgingly gave George room for only two of his songs, "Think for Yourself" and "If I Needed Someone." Ringo sat patiently on the sidelines, waiting to play his drum part, passing the time in mindless card games with Mal and Neil.

Working out a song in the studio with George Martin.

Paul's song "Michelle" was the romantic cornerstone of *Rubber Soul*, with lyrics in French as well as English. "Norwegian Wood" showcased the evolving musical strengths of John, Paul, and George, with John's wordplay, Paul's lyrical contributions, and George's first sitar solo.

John's other contributions on the album ranged from tender to angry, and laid bare his complicated feelings about women: "Girl" was melancholy, full of longing and remorse; in "Run for Your Life," jealousy and bitterness poured out as he sang that he'd rather see his girlfriend dead than with another man.

Inspired by Dylan, John tried writing a journalistic-style song for the album, naming all the sights he could see riding the bus from home to downtown. As he wrote, his lyrics felt repetitive and boring. John gave up and lay down. He was flooded with tender lyrics about the places and people he'd loved as a child. He considered the song ("In My Life") his first real literary piece of work. "Up till then it had all been sort of glib and throw-away," he said.

It had been a similar process when he'd tried to write "Nowhere Man." John had spent five hours trying to write a song that felt meaningful and gave up in frustration. Suddenly all the words and music for "Nowhere Man" came to him. "So letting it *go* is what the whole game is," John said. "You put your finger on it, it slips away, right?"

The Beatles did a short, eight-city tour in Britain with the release of *Rubber Soul* in December 1965, then were mercifully free of commitments for the next few months. John plunged full tilt into his newest fixation: LSD. Months earlier, he and Cynthia had joined George and Patti at a small dinner party where their host had slipped LSD into their coffee. The acid heightened their perceptions of everything, magnifying and distorting colors, sounds, and emotions. Frantic to get away, they'd jumped into George's Mini and driven to a nearby club. As the acid came on stronger, they began hallucinating—John was sure the club was on fire, but it turned out to be just a red light. "We were just *insane*," John said. "We were just out of our heads." For George, the experience was transcendent: God seemed to be everywhere. Cynthia was terrified, John captivated. He sought out more LSD, melting an acid-laced sugar cube on his tongue or eating a tiny, acid-drenched piece of blotter paper. He could take just a little lick or nibble for a "sparkle" or he could go on a full-blown trip, and as he came down, swallow more acid to take off again.

John headed out for the clubs at night, bringing all sorts of people back home to party. Cynthia would wake up to a house full of stoned, exhausted people, all wanting to be fed. She

The Beatles have breakfast on tour.

pleaded with John to think about his health, to be more careful, to consider what he was exposing Julian to. John refused to listen. She was miserable about how distant she and John were, but she couldn't reach him.

Ringo was the next to try LSD, and the three of them crowed to Paul about how wonderful it was, pressuring him to try it. Paul refused.

The effects of LSD showed up in April 1966, when they began putting together their next album, *Revolver*. They recorded "She Said, She Said," John's song about an experience he'd had the past August on the Beatles' most recent tour of America. At an outdoor party in Los Angeles, John had dropped acid. American musicians and movie stars mingled around the pool. The sun was shining, women were dancing. The actor Peter Fonda kept sidling up to John, sitting next to him and whispering, "I know what it's like to be dead, man." It freaked John out—he was tripping on acid and didn't want to know what it was like to be dead! But the phrase was burned into his mind and became part of the song's transcendent, mysterious message about death.

For inspiration for "Tomorrow Never Knows," John drew heavily on teachings from *The Tibetan Book of the Dead*. In the studio, he wanted a thousand chanting monks in the background, and asked George Martin to record his voice so that it sounded like the Dalai Lama chanting on a far-off hill. Martin ran John's voice through a speaker to distort it and added the drone of an

Indian tambour in lieu of the thousand chanting monks. He recorded on sixteen tape players, then played them back at different speeds or backward, to create a trippy, psychedelic sound.

This kind of manipulation was typical of what John expected from George Martin: to understand the concepts in his head and make them happen. In the studio John worked impatiently, ready to finish and move on to the next song. Paul was just the opposite. He would come into the studio with everyone's part carefully worked out, telling them exactly what he wanted. It took much more studio time for Paul to get precisely what he was imagining, as he made each musician do his part over and over again.

In the spring, John did a lengthy interview with Maureen Cleave, from the *London Evening Standard*. He spoke candidly to Maureen, a friend, and told her he had been reading extensively about religions. "Christianity will go. It will vanish and shrink," he said. "We're more popular than Jesus now." His remark was reprinted out of context on the front page of an American teen magazine, *Datebook*, on July 29, 1966, just before the Beatles were scheduled for their fourth American tour.

There was an immediate firestorm of protest, especially in the South. Radio stations banned their songs. Beatles records and John's books were heaped into huge piles and burnt across the Bible Belt.

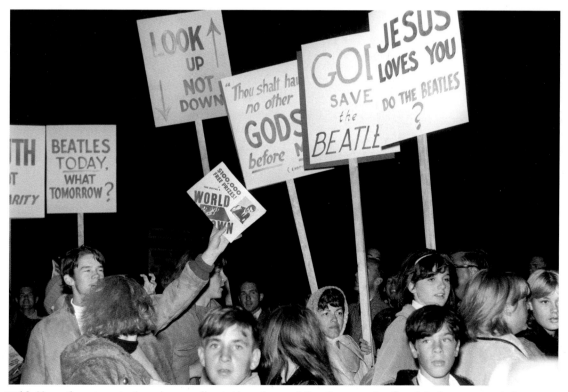

1966: More than twenty American radio stations banned Beatles records after John's controversial comment, and protestors turned out to picket Beatles concerts.

On August 5, 1966, Martin Luther King, Jr., (center) led a peaceful march protesting housing discrimination in Chicago. Angry white hecklers threw bottles, firecrackers, and rocks, hitting King in the head with a rock.

Brian rushed off to America to calm things down. Chicago, where the tour was scheduled to begin, was already on edge. On July 10, Martin Luther King, Jr., had addressed a crowd of more than fifty thousand people protesting discrimination. Over the summer he led marches into white neighborhoods, demanding that housing be opened up to blacks. The response from some whites was vitriolic. The city teetered on the edge of violence.

Frantic about the Beatles' safety, Brian considered canceling their trip. Onstage in those huge arenas they were incredibly vulnerable. "I thought they'd kill me—'cause they take things so seriously there," John said from England. "They shoot you, and then they realize it wasn't that important. . . . I was scared stiff." John, pressured by the others, reluctantly agreed to go, and to apologize on August 12 at their Chicago press conference.

It was agonizing. The press was hostile, ready to devour him. He was apprehensive as he faced the media and began a stumbling, evasive explanation. The reporters asked him bluntly if he was prepared to apologize. John, antagonized, answered belligerently. "I never meant it to be a lousy anti-religious thing. I apologize if that will make you happy. I still don't know quite what I've done. I've tried to tell you what I did do but if you want me to apologize, if that will make you happy, then OK, I'm sorry."

On that painful, dissonant note, the Beatles started their tour. Their new material was too complex to perform live. They were forced to rely on old standard hits, which were worn out and felt repetitious to them. Anonymous death threats rolled in, and the Klan ominously promised trouble. At the Washington, D.C., concert a few days into the tour, members of Prince George's County Ku Klux Klan, dressed in their robes, paraded out front. Brian and the Beatles worried about everything from high-powered rifles to lynching.

Offstage the Beatles were locked in hotel rooms with layers of security. George and John particularly hated it. They longed for the days they'd played at the Cavern, laughing and joking with the audience, playing music they loved in their black leather jackets.

Edgier than ever, John read the news being carried in every paper and on television: America had been involved in the Vietnam War for several years and now President Johnson had called for a new offensive with systematic bombings of Communist North Vietnam. If

John in his hotel room after publicly apologizing for his remark about Jesus.

Communism wasn't stopped in Vietnam, Johnson argued, it would inevitably spread to the rest of the world. What some Americans responded to on the nightly news wasn't the threat of Communism: They saw mothers keening over their wounded children and rice fields decimated by Agent Orange. On campuses and streets across the U.S., students were the first to mobilize into marches, sit-ins, and protests.

The United States government worked feverishly to silence the protests sweeping the nation. Legislation was proposed setting criminal penalties for "obstruction of the Vietnam war effort," and detailed files were started by the FBI on anyone who might be a threat to the government. Martin Luther King, Jr., was included.

A grandmother and child take cover in a field in Chu Lai, South Vietnam, as a battle rages near their home.

An American soldier rests against a truck in Hue, South Vietnam, with slogans scrawled on his helmet.

A policeman, nightstick ready, confronts a fallen demonstrator in Grant Park, Chicago. As the U.S. government showed no signs of leaving Vietnam, protests continued for years in cities across the United States.

Police forcibly remove a protestor from a hearing room in Washington, D.C., August 1966. The Un-American Activities Committee was investigating civil rights groups that demonstrated against the Vietnam War.

At their New York press conference, the Beatles broke their long silence on the Vietnam War. "We think of it every day," John said. "We don't like it. We don't agree with it. We think it's wrong." He and the other Beatles weren't joking and smiling as they had done so many times before. "The continual awareness of what was going on made me feel ashamed I wasn't saying anything," John explained afterwards. "I burst out because I could no longer play that game any more."

Before the final show of the tour, at San Francisco's Candlestick Park on August 29, 1966, the Beatles made a decision: They were done touring. It had become a dispiriting, exhausting grind, and now it was a dangerous one. John took a camera onstage with him and photo-graphed the other Beatles. "Nice working with you, Ringo," John cracked as they headed into their last number, "Long Tall Sally," a private, nostalgic tribute to the hundreds of times they'd played rock'n'roll together onstage. After more than fourteen hundred live performances, the Beatles had just played their last show.

They returned to England with a chasm looming before them. It was the first time in years their lives weren't hectically scheduled. They could go off on their own, without one another and the retinue of people pressing in on them.

Brian was devastated by their decision. After years of constant contact with all of the Beatles, there was suddenly little need to see them. His wide-swinging moods increased in intensity and he found it nearly impossible to sleep. He popped even more pills to cope.

Paul took off on a road safari across Africa, composed music for a film, and produced records for other artists. George, having played the Indian sitar on John's song "Norwegian Wood," decided to fully commit himself to learning the sitar. He and Patti, now married, traveled to Kashmir, India, where they were mesmerized by the religious ceremonies and holy men. Ringo settled in at home with his wife, Maureen, and their new baby, Zak.

John was terrified. Who was he without the other Beatles, without touring? Offered a small role in the movie *How I Won the War*, by Richard Lester, who had directed *A Hard Day's Night* and *Help!*, he jumped at the chance. On September 5, 1966, he flew to Germany for the film's first location, and the next day was given a regulation Army haircut and a pair of wire-frame glasses. He

John played Private Gripweed in Richard Lester's antiwar film How I Won the War. *Lester mixed the fictional death of his characters with horrifying documentary footage from WWII, offending some viewers.*

liked them. For the first time in his life, he left his glasses on in public. Beatle fans, seeing the photos of him, were shocked. What had happened to John's hair? And *glasses*?

But under the short hair and glasses, he was still the same John. Back home after weeks on location, John folded up on his small couch, daydreaming and half-watching TV, paying little attention to Cynthia and Julian. After dinner he sped out in his chauffeur-driven SS Mini Cooper to see what London's nightlife had to offer. He eagerly attended a "happening" at the Indica art gallery on November 9, thinking a "happening" might mean an orgy.

It didn't. As he walked in, John was handed a catalog for *Unfinished Paintings and Objects*. The catalog highlighted a big black bag with a "member of the audience inside," a TV screen set up to monitor the sky, and "a mirror to see your behind." As John moved around the gallery looking at the artwork, the artist, Yoko Ono, appeared, dressed all in black, with long black hair framing her face. She handed John a card with one word printed on it: BREATHE. He panted at her.

Yoko standing next to a sculpture by John Latham, 1967. She became friends with Latham, an avant-garde British artist interested in the fusion of art and science, when she moved to London in 1966.

Yoko took John on a tour of her artwork. Stopping before an empty canvas with a hammer hanging on a chain beside it, she told him that for five shillings he could hammer a nail into the canvas. John instantly understood the humor in her work, and offered her a pretend five shillings for a pretend nail. She invited him to climb a short ladder and look through a magnifying glass at the tiny letters written on a canvas on the ceiling. John climbed up and peered at the letters, which spelled out YES.

Yoko recognized a kind of electricity in the air between them. She began a determined attempt to get to know him better, and sent him a copy of her book, *Grapefruit: A Book of Instructions and Drawings.*

She followed *Grapefruit* with a series of postcards, some with only one word on them. John's emotions flipped back and forth as the postcards arrived. One minute he liked them, the next minute they seemed ridiculously avant-garde. Yoko began driving out unannounced to his house, hoping to see him.

Despite his fascination with LSD and his growing interest in Yoko, John had songs to write, albums to record. George Martin and Brian kept the pressure on John and Paul for new material. At home, John often composed at the piano, his fingers feeling out easy chords, his mind wandering, half listening to the TV muttering softly in the background. Sometimes he'd put odd, nonsensical words to chords and rhythms that captivated him. Often a phrase, stanza, or even the words to a full song swirled through his mind. He'd repeat the words over and over, developing a melody, fine-tuning the words. "I do get up from the piano," John said, "as if I have been in a trance."

Paul would drive out to Weybridge in the late morning, full of ideas and songs, some half-finished, some only in need of a bit of John's tight wordplay or his bluesy chords. They'd go up to John's music room to work together. "I don't like to do it in front of people," Paul explained. "It's like sex for me, I never was an orgy man."

As the complexity of their songwriting had increased, they tended to each work alone on a song, bringing it to the other in a more finished state. Their meetings were intense, collaborative, and confrontational. John would tear into Paul's songs. "We had great screaming sessions about them," Paul said. Paul gave back as good as he got. They were having a big blow-up one day when John took off his glasses, said, "It's only me, Paul," and put back on his glasses.

They went right back to fighting, their passionate competition fueling their songwriting.

Late in November 1966, the Beatles filed back into the studio, ready to put together another album. In the midst of the insanity and pressure of their career, John and Paul let off steam by sneaking references to sex and drugs into their music. Part of the challenge was seeing if they could get them past George Martin. "If we could put in something that was a little bit subversive then we would," Paul said. "George Martin might say, 'Was that "dit dit" or "tit tit" you were singing?' 'Oh, "dit dit" George, but it does sound a bit like that, doesn't it?' Then we'd get in the car and break down laughing."

They recorded Paul's "Penny Lane," a clear-eyed remembrance of the Liverpool they had all tramped around: the barbershop near the bus roundabout, the fire station, and the fish and chips shop. Just to get away with it, Paul slipped in "finger pie"—the illicit teenage pleasure he remembered of reaching a hand down a girl's pants.

John, inspired by Paul's song, and determined to do one better, came up with "Strawberry Fields Forever," a surreal song invoking the same 1950s Liverpool, named after the old Salvation Army girls' home where he used to play. John sang it through for a spellbound Martin, playing the simple, reflective melody on an acoustic guitar. "That wonderfully distinctive voice had a slight tremor," said Martin, "a unique nasal quality that gave his song poignancy, almost a feeling of luminescence. I was spellbound. I was in love."

Transformed in the studio by everyone's input, the song became more complex, weighed down by the drum and electric guitars. Martin put together a softer, orchestral version, adding cellos and trumpets. John liked the first half of one and the second half of the other, and casually told Martin to splice the two takes together. It was a nearly impossible task: They were in different keys, even different tempos. By slowing down the faster version, Martin got the pitch and tempo matched up. John was thrilled when it worked seamlessly. "He expected miracles," said Martin. "Sometimes he got them."

In the first six months of 1967, free of touring, the Beatles recorded thirteen more songs, logging hundreds of hours of studio time. No longer fueled by sheer, raw vitality, they were sophisticated, talented young men: John and Ringo were twenty-six, Paul and George, twenty-four. Deeply connected with one another musically and personally, they were functioning at the height of their creative power as a group.

At one studio session John gulped down a pill he thought was an upper. It was LSD. When the acid started coming on, he didn't know what was happening. "I just noticed all of a sudden I got so scared on the mike," John said. "I thought I was going cracked." Martin took him up on the flat roof, warning him to stay away from the edge. John noticed the stars were astonishingly brilliant. Finally it hit him: He'd taken acid. He returned to the session, but couldn't go on.

Paul drove John home and decided to join him tripping on acid. "I saw paisley shapes and weird things," said Paul, "and for a guy who wasn't that keen on getting that weird, there was a disturbing element to it." What made Paul's skin crawl was exactly what attracted John to LSD—a huge warping of reality, and an opening to all kinds of bizarre, psychedelic, unreal possibilities and connections.

The Beatles heard that Elvis, instead of going on the road himself, had sent his gold-plated Cadillac on tour. People had actually *paid* to admire his car. They decided, since they had sworn off touring, they'd send their next album out on tour.

In San Francisco, the Summer of Love was gearing up. Bands with long names like Country Joe and the Fish, Quicksilver Messenger Service, and Big Brother and the Holding Company, were playing in the parks and music halls. John and Paul came up with the impromptu band name Sergeant Pepper's Lonely Hearts Club Band, which became the title of their next album and its opening track. They began the first song on the album as if they were introducing a show, moved straight from song to song, sometimes without any pause between cuts, and ended with a wrap-up to close the "show." For the cover, the Beatles dressed in bright, satiny, military-style uniforms, pretending they *were* Sergeant Pepper's Band.

John's songs on the album were irreverent, angry, tender, and psychedelic. "Lucy in the Sky with Diamonds" sounded like an acid trip. Because of lyrics about newspaper taxis and tangerine skies, a rumor flew around that the title stood for LSD. John denied it—the title came from a picture four-year-old Julian had drawn of his friend Lucy with a starry sky behind her; the imagery was inspired by *Alice in Wonderland*.

Released June 1, 1967, *Sgt. Pepper's Lonely Hearts Club Band* instantly captured the psychedelic Summer of Love. People gathered to dance in the sun in free outdoor concerts, the sweet smell of marijuana smoke drifting lazily overhead. Speakers everywhere blared out *Sgt. Pepper*. It was happening. It was *now*. It was peace and love and freedom.

Everyone talked about the brilliantly enigmatic line, "I'd love to turn you on," in John's song "A Day in the Life." Did he mean grass? Acid? Sex? Something bigger and more cosmic?

"That was one of the great things about collaborating," Paul said. "You could nudge-nudge, wink-wink a bit, whereas if you're sitting on your own, you might not put it in. You know, 'I'd love to turn you on,' we literally looked at each other like, 'Oh, dare we do this?' It was a good moment, there was always good eye contact when we put those things in."

To some listeners, the Beatles' latest album held a promise of radical social change.

On May 19, 1967, Brian Epstein hosted a small press party at his Chapel Street home in London to celebrate the release of Sgt. Pepper.

"Hearing *Sgt. Pepper*, smoking reefers and planning the revolution in my friend's loft, we were just overwhelmed by their vision," said Abbie Hoffman in New York City. "It summed up so much of what we were saying politically, culturally, artistically, expressing our inner feelings and our view of the world in a way that was so revolutionary."

It was a huge weight for one album and four musicians to carry. At Brian's celebratory party for the album, John was in bad shape. He was smoking dope and dropping acid continually, eating and sleeping irregularly. He looked thin and exhausted.

In late August, George and Patti heard that a spiritual teacher from India, the Maharishi Mahesh Yogi, was giving a lecture in town. They talked the other Beatles into going with them. Fascinated by what the Maharishi was saying, the next day they all took the train to Bangor, Wales, for a ten-day spiritual conference.

The Maharishi introduced them to Transcendental Meditation. He gave them each a secret mantra to repeat and told them they only needed to meditate for half an hour every day. "What if you're greedy?" John asked. "And have another half hour's meditation after lunch, then slip in another half hour after tea?"

A few days into the conference, devastating news reached the Beatles: On August 27 Brian Epstein had been found dead in his bed, overdosed on prescription medications.

Caught in the crush of the press on their way back home, John looked dazed. He licked his lips nervously, his breathing rapid and shallow as he and the other Beatles fielded questions. John explained

John with the Maharishi, who introduced him to meditation.

The Beatles meeting the press after being told about Brian's death. Five weeks later they attended Brian's memorial at the New London Synagogue, a short walk from the EMI studios where Brian had first taken them to meet George Martin in 1962.

the Maharishi had counseled them not to be overwhelmed by grief but to keep their thoughts about Brian happy.

The sorrow and bewilderment etched into John's face made a lie of his words. It was an overwhelming loss for him in a lifetime of losses, complicated by another feeling: Having introduced Brian to pills, John felt an agonizing guilt for his death. He was also acutely aware that all the Beatles knew how to do was make music. Brian had handled all their business for them.

John thought to himself, "We've fuckin' had it."

9

CRASHING BIG-TIME

1967-1969

*"We are all in little boxes, and somebody has to go in and rip
your fuckin' head open for you to allow something else in."*

FOUR DAYS AFTER Brian's death, the Beatles met at Paul's house to figure out how to manage without him. In many ways, they'd outgrown Brian. He'd been critically important when they were a pack of scruffs, needing to be cleaned up, their show packaged, their schedule organized and expanded. But they'd changed dramatically since 1962. Instead of hiring a new manager, they decided to set up a company, Apple Corps., to handle their business.

Paul corralled the others into jumping right into shooting a film, *Magical Mystery Tour*. They took off on a rambling coach trip around England with three camera operators and a ragtag group of actors. John, cajoled by Paul, came along reluctantly. He only really engaged in the studio, recording one of his strangest, most fascinating songs, "I Am the Walrus," for the film and accompanying album.

The first two nights in the studio the Beatles taped sixteen takes of the rhythm track, then overdubbed bass, drums, and John's mesmerizing lead vocal. A few weeks later they recorded

Despite freezing cold weather, the Beatles filmed a surreal dinner sequence in Knole Park, about twenty miles southeast of London. As part of a promotion for "Strawberry Fields Forever" and "Penny Lane," the clip aired extensively around the world in 1967.

June 25, 1967: John getting ready to perform "All You Need Is Love" on the world's first global satellite TV broadcast, watched by more than 350 million people worldwide. In five words, "All You Need Is Love" summed up the philosophy of the sixties. Two weeks later, the single became a worldwide hit, and it appeared on The Magical Mystery Tour *album released in the U.S. on November 27, 1967.*

sixteen classical musicians playing Martin's orchestral score, and sixteen vocalists whooping, laughing, and blurting out John's inspired, silly lines: "Oompah, oompah, stick it up your jumper" and "Got one, got one, everybody's got one." "Weirdness is fine by me," Martin said, "in fact I loved the anarchy of John's thoughts—if I could fix and channel them."

Without someone like George Martin to channel the anarchy of John's *personal* thoughts, he was in a heavy, downward spiral, aided by his near-constant drug use. Brian's death only exacerbated John's fragile emotional state.

He often retreated to his music room, making strange, eclectic recordings of piano, guitar, vocals, comedy, and electronic music. They were just for his own sanity; he rarely let anyone else hear them.

John's disconnected feelings were profound. "If I am on my own for three days, doing nothing, I almost leave myself completely. I'm just not here," John explained. He felt he was either at the back of his head, or outside his body, watching himself. "I can see my hands and realize they're moving, but it's a robot who's doing it." Being with the other Beatles helped. "I have to see the others to see myself. I realize then there is someone else like me, so it's satisfying and reassuring. It's frightening really, when it gets too bad."

One night Cynthia and John attended a meditation class. Sitting quietly in the corner was Yoko, dressed all in black. Cynthia, seeing Yoko for the first time, suddenly felt very threatened. After the class as she and John stepped into their limo, Yoko slipped in with them. Cynthia looked at John in disbelief, but his face registered only surprise. They dropped Yoko off at her apartment, and a desperate, powerful intuition flooded Cynthia about John and Yoko. "When I first set eyes on Yoko I knew that she was the one for John. It was pure instinct; the chemistry was right; the mental aura that surrounded them was almost identical."

Soon Yoko sent John a package called *Mend Piece*. He opened it in front of Cynthia and her mother. Inside was a box of Kotex, with a broken red cup hidden among the clean, white sanitary pads.

Alarmed, Cynthia asked John what was going on. He insisted Yoko was just a nutty artist who was after money for her avant-garde art. He sponsored Yoko's art show *Half a Wind*, subtitled *Yoko and Me*. In return, Yoko opened the show on his twenty-seventh birthday.

In February 1968, John and Cynthia left Julian with Cynthia's mother and took off with the other Beatles and their wives to study with the Maharishi at Rishikesh, his retreat in the foothills of the Himalayas. John left England ebullient in his praise of the Maharishi—he was sure meditation and the Maharishi were *the* answer. "It's much better than acid," John said. "This is the biggest thing in my life now and it's come at the time when I need it most."

Instead of unwinding at Rishikesh, John was preoccupied and anxious. At seven every morning he shot out of the room he shared with Cynthia, saying he was going to meditate. It wasn't until later that she realized he was rushing off alone to collect the mail, looking for letters from Yoko. A steady stream of them came.

John spent hours alone every day writing songs, sitting with the Maharishi, or meditating on his own. For the first time in years, John was free of drugs and alcohol. The songs he wrote were exquisite, pulled out of the thin mountain air at Rishikesh. Many of them chronicled the devastatingly low moods that were hitting him. He felt lonely, desperate for a little peace of

John and Yoko in 1968.

mind, so suicidal he even hated his beloved rock'n'roll. He slipped his growing obsession with Yoko into "Julia," a song of tender yearning for his mother. Covering his real thoughts, he used the English translation of her name, writing that "Ocean Child" was calling to him.

After several months, a rumor flew around the retreat that the Maharishi had made sexual advances to one of the young women disciples. John wasn't sure what to believe. But when George, the most committed to meditation and the Maharishi, expressed concern the rumor might be true, John made an abrupt decision. He was done with India, done with the Maharishi, upset there was no easy answer and peace of mind. Along with the other Beatles, he packed up and left the next day, disillusioned.

Back in London, John threw himself into his former over-the-top drug use, completely shut off from Cynthia. Thinking John needed room to sort out all the changes happening in his life, she left Julian in the housekeeper's care and joined friends on a Greek holiday.

The last night Cynthia was gone, John invited Yoko over. He was nervous, unsure of himself. He took her up to his music room and played his tapes for her. They spent the night recording, improvising, flirting, collaborating. As the sun rose they made love.

John realized immediately that his marriage was over. He wanted only to be with Yoko. "It was very beautiful," John said. "I had no doubt I'd met The One."

Cynthia returned home around four in the afternoon. The house was quiet, the shades still drawn. She found John and Yoko sitting in the morning room dressed only in bathrobes. John and Yoko welcomed her casually, as if nothing was amiss. Cynthia rushed out of the room, threw together a few things, and ran from the house.

As a young child, Yoko grew up with one foot in Japan and one in America: By the time she turned twelve, she had spent nearly five years in the United States. A lonely child full of unusual ways of seeing the world, Yoko was born into a Japanese family of enormous wealth and prestige: One grandfather was president of the Japan Industrial Bank and the other served in the upper house of the Japanese parliament. When Yoko was born on February 18, 1933, her father was working in San Francisco as a banking executive. They didn't meet until she was two, when her mother, Isoko, took her to the United States.

When she was a toddler, the servants were instructed not to help Yoko up if she fell: Her mother felt it was important she learn to help herself. Yoko ate her meals alone, sitting at a long table, with one of her tutors sitting silently next to her. "I had one private tutor who read me the bible," said Yoko, "and another foreign tutor who gave me piano lessons, and my attendant taught me Buddhism." Yoko's mother played shamizen and koto, traditional Japanese instruments, and knew several archaic vocal styles. Her father loved Western classical music, and Yoko was taught Eastern and Western music theory and harmony.

Between sojourns in America, Yoko was free to wander the huge family garden in Tokyo, where eight gardeners kept the grounds beautifully groomed. When the servants took her out in public, they were instructed to carry cotton and alcohol and swab down everything Yoko might touch.

The long American stay in the mid-thirties was followed by a second in 1941. Isoko took

Yoko and her younger brother, Keisuke, born when Yoko was three, to visit their father, now working in New York. They stayed for more than a year and Yoko attended public school in Scarsdale. Back in Japan with American clothes and attitudes, Yoko was sent to the most prestigious private school in Tokyo, Gakushuin, which only admitted students of noble blood. Emperor Hirohito's son, Akihito, the crown prince, was in Yoko's class.

Two months before Pearl Harbor, Isoko gave birth to another daughter, Setsuko. Despite America's frequent bombardment of Tokyo, Isoko felt safe in their bomb shelter in the garden, until the night of March 9, 1945, when American B-20s dropped thousands of incendiary bombs on the city. By dawn more than eighty thousand people were dead and one fourth of the city was destroyed.

Burnt tree branches and radio towers rise above the rubble of Tokyo after repeated American bombing. Incendiary bombs sometimes contained napalm and were used to burn more than 40 square miles of Tokyo in March 1945, while Yoko and her family hid in a bomb shelter all night. In the morning they saw the horrific destruction around them and evacuated to the countryside for safety.

Isoko fled to the countryside with her children, where they lived with farmers, struggling to get enough to eat. Taunted by the farm children as *bata kusai,* "smelling like butter," because she was from the city and ate Western foods, Yoko and her brother would often hide away inside for the afternoon, watching the sky through a hole in the roof, making up imaginary menus.

As Tokyo was rebuilding after the war, Yoko impressed her teachers, reading complex books in English, writing long pieces when she'd been asked for short essays. Like all the other high schoolers, she wore a uniform to school and bowed respectfully to her teachers.

While her mother insisted on proper behavior from her daughter, she had strong opinions about women's position in society. "She used to tell me that even a woman could become a diplomat or prime minister if she was as bright as I," Yoko said. "She also said I should not be so foolish as to get married or that I should not be foolish enough to have children." Her mother also warned her against smiling too often, as it might be considered a sign of weakness.

In 1952, Yoko was admitted to Gakushuin University, but, disillusioned, she dropped out after two semesters. Her mother and younger siblings had moved to New York, and Yoko decided to join her family in Scarsdale and go to Sarah Lawrence College. But she quickly found she wasn't happy living with her parents or going to Sarah Lawrence. She often spent time alone, lighting matches and watching the flames disappear, worried she was a pyromaniac.

She found a kindred spirit in Toshi Ichiyanagi, a student of classical piano at Juilliard who shared her enthusiasm for avant-garde music. They eloped and moved to an unheated fifth-floor loft downtown on the west side of Manhattan. Estranged from her family and overwhelmed with shyness, she wished she had a big box with tiny holes in it, so she could see out but nobody could see her. She wrote poetry and painted, but she felt like a misfit. She didn't know how to say to people what she was really doing: just holding on, trying not to go crazy or disappear. "So I just imagined myself holding on to a kite," she said, "and the kite was me." At night she would lose hold of the string and go floating away.

The New York art world Yoko wanted to find her way into was in the midst of a radical change. After the horrors of WWII, many artists wanted their work to be more than just beautiful: They wanted it to be meaningful socially and spiritually. Zen thought, with its meditative emphasis on *being in the moment* rather than *doing something*, appealed to many of the artists, including Yoko. Life itself was art.

Yoko began to put together art shows and staged performances to express her fear of disappearing or floating away. In *Match Piece*, she lit matches onstage, and, along with the audience, watched the flames burn out. She collaborated with avant-garde musicians like jazz saxophonist Ornette Coleman and composer John Cage, who believed all noises—and silence—were part of music. Her exhibitions featured a series of instructional paintings, including *Smoke Painting*, where people could light a match and watch the smoke billow against the canvas, and *Painting to Be Stepped On*, which was laid on the floor and became a crisscrossed canvas of footprints.

But she wasn't a perfect fit in the avant-garde music scene as she wailed, groaned, and howled her improvised voice parts with Cage and others. She felt that the musicians were aesthetic and asexual. She was willing to tear herself open emotionally, desperate to express the anger boiling inside her. "I wanted to throw blood," she said.

In March 1962, Yoko returned to Tokyo, joining her husband, Toshi, who had moved back to Japan in the fall. Though she staged concerts and exhibitions in Tokyo's experimental art community, she felt isolated and deeply depressed.

She thought constantly about killing herself. In the middle of the night, not fully awake, she would get out of bed and walk over to the window of their eleventh-floor apartment. But before she could fall from the open window, Toshi would always grab her and pull her away. Finally she was checked into a sanitarium, where she was kept heavily sedated.

Released several months later, she left Toshi and married Anthony Cox, a visiting New York jazz musician and film producer. Tony, awed by Yoko's talent, began producing Yoko's exhibitions and performances. On August 8, 1963, she and Tony had a baby girl, Kyoko. They returned to New York City, where the responsibility for Kyoko fell mostly to Tony. Yoko considered herself the more creative one in the marriage, and insisted on being free of the daily needs of a small child.

Yoko and Tony quickly developed a reputation in New York for staging interesting exhibitions of Yoko's art—different, offbeat, often requiring participation from the audience. In *Cut Piece*, she sat onstage wearing a black dress, and invited audience members to cut off

Photo by Peter Moore © Estate of Peter Moore/VAGA, New York

March 21, 1965: Yoko performed Cut Piece *at the Carnegie Recital Hall in New York City. She had previously staged the event twice in Japan during the summer of 1964. Yoko noticed that Americans were not as discreet about cutting off her dress as the Japanese.*

pieces of her clothing. She sat completely still, staring straight ahead, as people came up one by one, picked up the scissors, and cut. Yoko was embarrassed and frightened, but she staged *Cut Piece* in the Zen tradition of choosing something difficult and watching herself as she dealt with it.

In 1964, Yoko published *Grapefruit*. She felt the book was a cure. "It was like saying, 'Please accept me, I am mad,'" she said. "As long as you are behaving properly, you don't realize your madness and you go crazy."

With Tony's experience in films, they put together a movie in 1965, *Bottoms*, a parade of naked butts. *Bottoms* created a buzz for Yoko: Her work was met with interest, excitement, incomprehension, even hostile skepticism. In 1966, she and Tony moved to London to take part in the Destruction of Art Symposium in London. Yoko's *Cut Piece* was a hit. "It was impossible," wrote one reviewer, "to disentangle the compulsion of the audience to cut and Yoko Ono's compulsion to be cut." Despite Tony and Kyoko, and Yoko's popularity in the avant-garde art scene, her old feelings of being isolated and lonely swept over her.

Enter John Lennon. Still in an acid-induced stage of ego destruction, he needed Yoko as much as she needed him. From the moment they first made love, they were inseparable: two brilliant, eccentric, self-centered, alienated people who no longer felt alone in the world. Within a few days they moved into an apartment in London together, leaving Julian with Cynthia and Kyoko with Tony.

John brought Yoko to the studio when the Beatles met a few weeks later on May 30, 1968, to make *The Beatles,* commonly called the "White Album." The first song they recorded was John's "Revolution 1." The Summer of Love and nonviolent protest had devolved into bloody confrontations worldwide. In Paris, thousands of students had clashed with police on "Bloody Monday," turning the Boulevard St. Germain into a battleground. In the United States, Martin Luther King, Jr., had been assassinated on April 4, and fiery riots broke out in more than a hundred cities. As President Johnson committed ever-increasing troops to Vietnam—by now, nearly half a million—militant, angry antiwar activists flooded campuses and city streets.

Some of the "Revolution" recording was pure chaos. Over the jamming, feedback-filled guitar parts, John screamed "all right" over and over again, while Yoko, joining the Beatles in the studio for the first time, moaned and talked on-microphone with John. The message in his verses was contradictory—if there was to be destructive revolution, he wanted to be counted out . . . and in.

From this moment on, Yoko came to virtually every recording session with John, sitting next to him, whispering comments and criticisms in his ear. He listened and encouraged her. Repeating to the others what she'd said, he expected them to make the changes she suggested. Sure they would find Yoko as astonishing and sexy as he did, John jealously warned Paul not to make a pass at her.

No chance. The other Beatles resented John's fanatical insistence on Yoko's constant presence. She'd broached the sanctity of the Beatles' four-cornered fort in their most private spot: the recording studio. The others felt self-conscious, inhibited, and angry. The sessions became so tense that steady, easygoing Ringo quit the group in August and had to be cajoled back into the studio more than a week later.

But Yoko opened John up to a world beyond Beatles music: She offered him access to the avant-garde art scene, a world of edgy creation, possibility, and expansion. It was also, to John's relief, a world that didn't worship the Beatles or insist that he be one of the loveable "moptops." John immediately began staging "events" with Yoko. As part of the National Sculpture Exhibition in June, they planted two acorns outside Coventry Cathedral. They opened an exhibit on July 1 with the release of 365 helium-filled balloons. Over the next

Yoko and John opened their 1968 art exhibit, "You Are Here," with the release of 365 helium balloons. Each balloon bore a small card asking the finder to write back to John. In the gallery John had amassed collection boxes in the shapes of disabled children and animals, commonly used in England to collect coins for various charities.

*The Beatles' full-length animation feature,
Yellow Submarine, was released in July 1968.
The Beatles contributed four previously
unreleased songs, appeared in a live-action
sequence at the end of the film, and showed up
for the premiere. Beatles imitators supplied
the dialogue after the Beatles decided not to
participate in the recording.*

months, they made avant-garde films: *Smile*, *Two Virgins*, *Rape*, and *Self Portrait*, a slow-motion
film of John's penis in various degrees of erection. There was no mention of *Self Portrait* in the
media. "The critics wouldn't touch it," Yoko said later.

While John and Yoko's creative lives were in blissful ferment, their personal lives were in
turmoil. The police showed up at their apartment on October 18, 1968, with a search
warrant and found a small amount of marijuana. A week later Yoko and John announced they
were expecting a baby, but on November 21 Yoko miscarried.

A week after the miscarriage, John pleaded guilty to unlawful possession of cannabis and
was fined. While still reeling from all these difficulties, he and Yoko released *Unfinished Music
No. 1: Two Virgins*, the avant-garde sounds they had recorded their first night together. The
cover, a picture of the two of them nude, caused an uproar.

October 19, 1968: John and Yoko leaving the Marylebone Magistrates' Court, where John was charged with possession of cannabis.

With all of John's creative energy going into projects with Yoko, Paul struggled to keep the Beatles moving forward. Despite being deeply in love with a new woman, Linda Eastman, Paul was unable to understand John's need to be with Yoko twenty-four hours a day. John even insisted on Yoko's involvement when he and Paul were writing songs together.

In early January 1969, Paul rounded everyone up and got them back in the studio to record a new album. With the band on the verge of collapse, Paul lobbied hard to get the others to tour again. When that idea failed, they reluctantly agreed to have all their studio time filmed. Paul hoped a movie might come out of it.

With Yoko at his side, John recorded "Across the Universe," a song he'd written while still living with Cynthia. The lyrics were full of transcendent, free-floating imagery—broken light, undying love, and words slithering across the universe—evoking a fragile sense of peace. He designed his melody around the lyrics, giving each verse its own unique rhythmic pattern.

"It *drove* me out of bed," he said later about the song. "I didn't want to write it, I was just slightly irritable and I went downstairs and I couldn't get to sleep until I put in on paper, and then I went to sleep."

In the studio, tensions ricocheted through the group. Paul dominated the others, and Yoko's constant presence kept the four Beatles from hitting their stride. Sessions were set to start in the morning, a time when John was far from his most creative. The addition of a film crew shooting the sessions made it almost impossible to achieve the intimacy and connection they needed.

The four of them bickered, their music sometimes out of tune and off tempo. They did a lot of jamming, moved from song to song, finding it difficult to focus on finishing anything. George, after being told what to do one too many times by Paul, walked out and only returned after a long, difficult meeting with the others. The emotional fluidity the Beatles depended on with one another was gone.

Listening to a playback in January 1969.

In the studio, John was bleary-eyed, disengaged. The others soon realized he and Yoko were strung out. "The two of them were on heroin, and this was a fairly big shocker for us," said Paul, "because we all thought we were far-out boys but we kind of understood that we'd never get quite that far out."

George Martin was sure the group was self-destructing. "This is the end," he thought. "I don't want to be part of this anymore." On January 22, George and Paul were just about to duck into the studio when they ran into organ player Billy Preston. In town playing with Ray Charles, Billy had known all of them since 1962 when he was a teenage member of Little Richard's band and they'd shared a two-week booking in Hamburg at the Star-Club. George grabbed Billy and brought him into the studio. With Billy's expansive, warm personality and sustaining keyboard playing pulling the music together, the atmosphere of the sessions immediately improved.

The film crew, eager to shoot a live performance, talked the Beatles into playing together on the roof of their office building. The day was cold and windy as the Beatles trouped up to the roof on January 30. They picked up their instruments, and began. "Once the count-in happened," Ringo said, "we turned back into those brothers and musicians." For forty-two minutes they slipped into a groove with one another: Ringo's drumming was tight, Paul's singing exuberant, George's guitar masterful. John wisecracked and quipped with Paul, and when he forgot some of the words to "Don't Let Me Down," he bluffed his way through, just as he had so many years ago as a teenager when Paul had first seen him at the Woolton church fete.

ABOVE: Billy Preston was such an excellent keyboardist, the Beatles had him record an impromptu solo on "Get Back." OVERLEAF: The Beatles' last live performance, on the roof of the Apple headquarters in London on January 30, 1969.

Despite their fabulous performance on the rooftop, no one could figure out how to pull an album out of the inconsistent recording they'd done. The project was shelved and not released for more than a year.

They ran headlong into another serious problem: The business they had set up to handle their affairs, Apple Corps., was crashing down on them. Over Paul's adamant objections, John, George, and Ringo appointed a coarse, rough-edged New York City accountant, Allen Klein, as their new business manager. Paul, now married to Linda, wanted to hire his new father-in-law, Lee Eastman, a conservative, old-money New Yorker.

Despite being in the majority on the new manager, John felt like he was submerging, giving in to Paul and letting him run everything. He resented Paul's efforts to keep the Beatles moving forward. "I was slowly putting meself together after Maharishi, bit by bit, over a two year period," he said. "I didn't believe I could do *anything*. I let Paul do what he wanted. . . . And I just was nothing, I was *shit*."

On a weekend visit to Derek Taylor, the Beatles' press agent, John dropped acid; it was strong stuff. In his fragile state, with his life in upheaval and too many drugs in his system, the acid devastated him. "I got a message on acid that you should destroy your ego," John said, "and I did." Derek sat up all night with him going through his life, going over the songs he'd written, reassuring him that he done important work, telling him not to be frightened.

The next weekend John dropped acid again, this time with Yoko. "She freed me completely, to realize that I was *me* and it's alright. And that was it. I started fighting again and being a loudmouth again and saying, 'Well I can do this,' and 'Fuck you, and this is what *I* want.'"

John had the same confidence-building effect on Yoko. "I'm starting to think that maybe I can live," she said. "Before, it seemed impossible; I was just about at the vanishing point, and all my things were too conceptual. But John came in and said, 'All right, I understand you.'"

It surprised everyone when the Beatles went back into the studio in July 1969 to record *Abbey Road*. It had only been a few months since their dismal wrap-up on *Let It Be*. Martin insisted the Beatles quit squabbling so much if they wanted his help. As always, Yoko was with John continually.

In spite of the tensions and flare-ups, the Beatles managed to keep their animosity submerged long enough to pull together an album. John and Paul, both hurt and angry, were

August 8, 1969: The Beatles waiting a few yards from the EMI recording studio to be photographed for the cover of their album Abbey Road. The image of them crossing the street in the "zebra crossing" became one of their best-known covers.

openly critical of each other's work. The four Beatles met together to lay down the main tracks, then did most of the overdubbing individually. John was especially pleased with his song "Come Together," done in the studio using a basic Chuck Berry riff from "You Can't Catch Me." With Ringo's tom-toms giving the song its heartbeat, the three guitars and an electric piano wove unrestrained harmonies around John's cryptic, humorous lyrics. "It's funky, it's bluesy, and I'm singing it pretty well," he said proudly. "You can dance to it."

The finished album had a polished, joyful sheen of Beatles magic. But by the time *Abbey Road* was released at the end of September 1969, the Beatles were no longer functioning as a band.

10

JOHNANDYOKO

1969–1971

"I'm not the Beatles, I'm me."

AS SOON AS their divorces were final, John and Yoko flew to Gibraltar, a British territory on the southern tip of Spain, and were married in a quick, private ceremony on March 20, 1969. Knowing they'd never get away from the press, they turned their honeymoon into an event, announcing they would hold a weeklong "Bed-in for Peace" at the Amsterdam Hilton. That brought dozens of reporters on the run to see what would happen. To the immense disappointment of the press, John and Yoko gave nonstop interviews on only one subject: their latest passion, peace.

In the months following their bed-in, they staged a series of happenings, not all of them as serious. Evoking Yoko's earlier desire for a box she could hide in and see out of, they called a press conference and never emerged from inside a big bag. They called it "Bagism," and the press struggled to understand the significance. John confided to a friend, "We were just pissing ourselves laughing inside that thing."

On April 22, 1969, John officially changed his name, adding a new middle name: Ono. He wanted to drop Winston, with its implication that he, like Churchill, was a staunch believer in the British Empire. On the day of the ceremony he was informed that he could add a name, but

Yoko and John admiring a Polaroid snapshot of themselves as newlyweds, on the flight back from Gibraltar, where they married on March 20, 1969.

not renounce one. Standing on the roof of the Apple headquarters on Savile Road in London, with Yoko at his side, he legally became John Winston Ono Lennon.

Besides being a headline-catching event, changing his name was a clear demonstration to Yoko how intensely he loved her. It also was proof he understood her feminism: She was willing to change her name for him, so he would do the same for her. For the first time in his life, John recognized a woman as outrageous, imaginative, smart, and powerful as he was. His feelings for her were intense and consuming. "When you actually are in love with somebody, you tend to be jealous. And want to own them, possess them 100 percent, which I do," he said. "I love Yoko. I want to possess her completely."

When people didn't immediately admire Yoko, John took it personally and threw the blame back at them. During a recording session, George had complained to John and Yoko about her constant presence. "We both sat through it," said John, "and I didn't hit him. I don't know why." If someone greeted him and not Yoko, it would incense him. He even blamed their heroin use on other people's attitudes. "We get into so much pain that we have to do something about it,"

In mid-May, 1969, John and Yoko decided to hold a second bed-in in New York. U.S. authorities refused to grant John a visa, so he and Yoko, with Kyoko in tow, flew to the Bahamas. Since John found the tropical climate too hot and humid to stay in bed for a week, they headed for Montreal, Canada, where American reporters could easily visit and broadcast their peace message back in the U.S.

Montreal bed-in, 1969. John sketched two sets of images of himself and Yoko on his guitar.

John said. "We took 'H' [heroin] because of what the Beatles and others were doing to us."

On May 26 John and Yoko climbed back into bed for another weeklong "Bed-in for Peace" in Montreal, Canada. Besides giving hundreds of interviews, John recorded his song "Give Peace a Chance," on a borrowed tape recorder. It was quintessential John Lennon magic: He managed to capture the essence of their peace quest in a clever, catchy, and satisfying song.

The first solo single record put out by a Beatle, "Give Peace a Chance" was released worldwide at the end of June. Though Paul had nothing to do with the song, John credited it to Lennon/McCartney as he had done with all his songs since he and Paul had begun writing together. John dubbed the eclectic backup group of singers the Plastic Ono band. This "group" was a conceptual brainwave—a band with no fixed members.

In August, John and Yoko moved into a new home, Tittenhurst Park, a seventy-four-acre estate with a sixteen-room mansion, in Ascot, just a few miles north of London. John, as usual, settled into the kitchen and a small room off it.

One of the first things he and Yoko did was to get off heroin. They locked themselves in their bedroom and quit cold turkey—abruptly stopping the heroin and going through painful withdrawal, agitated and exhausted, but unable to sleep. John captured the experience in "Cold Turkey," his voice careening between steel-edged and plaintive.

In September, shortly after recording *Abbey Road*, the Beatles met at Apple to sign a new record contract. They bantered uncomfortably—where were they heading as a band? Paul thought they needed to go back on the road and do small gigs again, get back to their roots. John looked at Paul and said bluntly, "Well, I think yer daft! . . . I'm leaving the group." He told them he wanted a divorce, just like he'd had from Cynthia. The others were stunned. After years as the most famous member of the world's most famous rock'n'roll band of all time, John no longer wanted to be Beatle John. He was, as he now often signed his name, *JohnandYoko*.

Klein insisted the four Beatles remain utterly tight-lipped about their impending breakup because of delicate business talks, as well as the upcoming releases of *Abbey Road* and *Let It Be*. John kept his mouth shut, but full of displeasure and rebelliousness, he returned his MBE medal to the queen on November 25. He wrote a short note, saying he was returning his MBE to protest Britain's involvement in the Nigeria-Biafra conflict and Britain's support of the American war in Vietnam, and because "Cold Turkey" was slipping down the music charts. Mimi was mortified, and furious with John.

Workmen finish putting up John and Yoko's Christmas peace message on a billboard in New York's Times Square, December 15, 1969.

At the end of the year, Yoko and John flew to Denmark to be with Kyoko, Tony, and his new wife, Melinda, on a remote farm with no phone. For the first few weeks they spent their days quietly, meditating and fasting. But it was too quiet for John and Yoko. They had a phone line installed, and immediately problems and hassles burst in on them. People called relaying grievances and rumors of what the other Beatles were doing, and how John and Yoko's latest new concept of a musical peace festival in Canada had become mired in anger, accusation, and back-stabbing. John had everyone fly in from Canada, Britain, and New York to try to sort it out. He struggled to keep control of the plans as more people appeared at the farm, uninvited, insisting on inserting their opinions.

The festival to promote peace derailed into a chaotic, ego-infested mess, as people shouted insults at one another. John was sick of chaos, tired of his musical career being out of his control. He and Yoko bailed on the whole idea. If they couldn't control the festival, they didn't want to be involved.

A few weeks after John's announcement to the other Beatles that he wanted a divorce, Paul had also fled London. With nerves stretched to the breaking point, he retreated to High Park Farm, an isolated farm in Scotland he had bought to escape the pressures of Beatlemania. For the first time in his life, Paul couldn't pull himself together. He lay awake at night, shaking, and didn't want to get out of bed in the morning. When he did finally get up, he didn't bother to shave. He headed straight for the bottle and had a drink.

Paul, photographed by his wife Linda, shortly after the breakup of the Beatles in 1970.

Paul's leaving the Beatles was front page news on April 10, 1970.

He was at a loss, betrayed by John, trapped by contracts, stuck with Klein.

The cure for Paul was making more music. He couldn't bear to be away from it for long. With Linda's help he put together his first solo album, *McCartney*. Out of touch with what was happening at Apple, he was furious when he discovered John had called in music producer Phil Spector to pull together the *Let It Be* tracks. Spector, famous for adding his "Wall of Sound" to rock records, added harps, horns, an orchestra, and a women's choir to Paul's song "The Long and Winding Road." That was upsetting enough, but when Paul was told the release date of *McCartney* would have to be delayed to get *Let It Be* out first, he fought back. He forced Apple to stick to his original release date, April 17, 1970, and to schedule *Let It Be* for May 8. Included in Paul's solo album was a written question-and-answer interview. He made it clear the Beatles were finished. The Lennon/McCartney partnership was over.

The press went wild. The breakup hit the front page of newspapers worldwide and led off television and radio reports. John was furious at being scooped. He called a press conference and said Paul couldn't quit the band because he'd fired him already. Their slagging match got full-on media coverage. Paul responded poignantly in an interview: "John's in love with Yoko and he's no longer in love with the other three of us."

Someone had to take the blame. The press agreed with Paul: The problem was Yoko. If she hadn't put the move on John, he would never have gone through his inexplicable avant-garde phase, and the Beatles—and even John's marriage to Cynthia—would still be intact. Coverage on Yoko was spiteful, filled with racist slurs. Letters of hatred poured into the

Apple office. It was the beginning of a long, bitter divorce, filled with suits and countersuits, as the Beatles sought to disentangle their contractual obligations and deal with hurt, angry feelings.

In the midst of the public furor over the Beatle breakup, John was given a book, *The Primal Scream*, by Arthur Janov. John was fascinated by Janov's psychotherapy, which he called "Primal Therapy." Participants would lie on the floor and remember an important, "primal" event in their childhood. Encouraged to live through it all over again—with full feeling— they'd end up crying, howling, screaming with anger and pain, whimpering.

In late April 1970, John and Yoko left for Los Angeles to do work with Janov. Taken back to relive pivotal moments in his childhood, John pushed past his tough exterior. "The sharp-talking king of the world was actually a terrified guy who didn't know how to cry," John said about himself. "Simple. Now I can cry."

John and Yoko stayed for four months, "primaling" alone or in a small group. But when Janov decided to shoot footage of John's group, John was furious. Janov swore it just *happened* to be John's group: John was certain Janov wanted footage of him.

They headed back to England where John used the intense vulnerability, fear, and anger he'd connected with to fuel a new, autobiographical album, *John Lennon / Plastic Ono Band*. He opened the first song, "Mother," with the deep, mournful tolling of a funeral bell. His voice was yearning and raw as he sang about the mother he wanted who hadn't wanted him.

John's songs knocked down a litany of idols (Jesus, Kennedy, Buddha, even the Beatles), lamented how isolated he and Yoko felt, and slammed The System for anesthetizing people with sex, religion, and TV. The final cut, "My Mummy's Dead," was one stanza, stripped down to the essential feelings of loss he had about his mother. To John, the song was like a haiku poem, its deceptive simplicity giving it tremendous power.

Poignantly aware of the absence of his father during his childhood, John made an attempt to reach out to his son, Julian. Janov had suggested he see Julian more often, and alone. John called Cynthia and arranged to spend several hours with Julian, now seven years old. He and Julian disappeared into Julian's room, chatting and drawing on Julian's chalkboard. John was cheerful and friendly with Cynthia, less guarded than he had been around her since their separation. He gave Cynthia a copy of *Primal Scream*, and told her he felt guilty about not seeing more of Julian.

Shortly after her divorce from John was final, Cynthia married hotel owner Robert Bassanini, shown here with Cynthia and seven-year-old Julian on their wedding day in the summer of 1970.

At first, Cynthia was hopeful that John and Julian would have a closer relationship, but John rarely made time again to be with Julian as he pursued his absorbing new life with Yoko. "My thing is, Out of sight, out of mind," John said. "That's my attitude towards life."

The press continued to blame Yoko for the breakup of the Beatles as well as his marriage to Cynthia. In December 1970, *Esquire* magazine ran an article with the shocking title, "John Rennon's Excrusive Gloupie."

While John was busy with Yoko and with recording his new album, Paul was growing increasingly upset with the power Klein had over him. He found there was only one way out of his contract: He had to sue the other Beatles. He agonized over the decision, finally deciding to go through with the lawsuit. On February 18, 1971, Paul filed a writ in the chancery division of the high court calling for the dissolution of the Beatles' partnership. The trial lasted nine days. Paul attended every day, dressed in a suit. The others never showed up. Paul won the case, severing his ties with Klein and with the other Beatles.

In the spring of 1971, John and Yoko immersed themselves in politics. They appeared at rallies and marches and gave money to radical causes. Once rock'n'roll itself had been revolutionary to John. "We needed something loud and clear to break through all the unfeeling and repression that had been coming down on us kids," he said. Now, rock'n'roll was moving into a more powerful sphere as John and other musicians realized they could mix politics with music to inspire people and create change.

Around the world, the streets were full of marchers, fists thrust high in the air, yelling "Power to the people!" John grabbed the phrase, and the emotional punch it packed, and in March 1971 released an unequivocally political song, "Power to the People."

Yoko, eager to see Kyoko again, found she was unable to locate Tony. He and Kyoko had slipped away, leaving no idea of their whereabouts. Yoko and John hired private investigators who finally ran Tony down in Majorca, Spain, in April 1971. John and Yoko flew to Majorca, approached seven-year-old Kyoko on her school playground, and whisked her away to their hotel. Tony immediately called the police, who moved in on John and Yoko before they could leave the island. For fourteen hours they were detained on suspicion of kidnapping. Yoko was incensed—how could a mother possibly kidnap her own daughter? The judge resorted to the same strategy that Freddie and Julia had used so many years before with five-year-old John: Which parent would she like to go with?

Kyoko chose her father.

Peace-loving John was furious. "We've done everything we can to come to an amiable agreement with the father," he declared. "Yoko loves her daughter, and I can't let her suffer like this any longer. What effect can all this be having on Kyoko?" He had painful memories of being asked to make the same choice. "I was shattered," he said.

John and Yoko returned to England without Kyoko. Rounding up a brilliant group of musicians in the studio they'd built at Tittenhurst Park, they focused on recording. John called in Phil Spector, who'd salvaged the *Let It Be* tapes, to produce. Yoko worked on her new album, *Fly*, while John recorded *Imagine*.

To put the finishing touches on their albums, John and Yoko flew to New York City. They hired string and sax players and booked time at the Record Plant studio with its sophisticated four-track recording equipment. While they were in New York, John received a call from George. He was putting together a benefit concert for flood-ravaged Bangladesh. Word had flown around the rock music community, and many musicians were eager to perform. George turned most of them down, knowing exactly who he wanted. Ringo was coming, Leon Russell, Eric Clapton, and Billy Preston. George hoped John would join them, but only John. He was adamant: no Yoko.

John was in a terrible bind. The concert was on everyone's minds. Tickets sold out in three

George Harrison and Bob Dylan perform at the Bangladesh benefit concert at Madison Square Garden, New York, August 1, 1971. Other performers included Ringo, Billy Preston, Eric Clapton, Ravi Shankar, and Leon Russell. The concert was Dylan's return to live performance after a long absence. John didn't appear.

hours when it was announced. John wanted to be part of it, but he knew Yoko would be devastated at not being invited. As soon as he put down the phone, he and Yoko got into a screaming fight. John stormed out of the hotel. Yoko waited, furious and hurt, but he didn't return.

The next morning Allen Klein called and told Yoko that John had been phoning him all night. He'd flown back to England and was at Tittenhurst Park, miserable. She needed to go to him right away. Yoko said no. He'd walked out on her.

Hours later, she relented and flew to London. She thought John would be at the airport. He wasn't. Nor was he in front of the house when she pulled up. She found him in the bedroom, kneeling inside one of their big bags. He apologized, but the incident upset Yoko. She was afraid it would happen again and the relationship might no longer be strong enough to withstand it.

When *Imagine* was released, it came as a shock to many people: It was tender, sincere, and haunting with its themes of personal pain and loss. In "Crippled Inside," John sang about how impossible it was to hide a feeling of being crippled, not physically, but on the inside. Many of the songs celebrated his love of Yoko, his profound need for her, even his deep regret over hurting her in a jealous rage.

The album also included a little rock'n'roll nastiness as John took a vicious swipe at Paul in "How Do You Sleep?" John's voice stung with contempt as he responded to what he saw as digs at him on Paul's recent record, *Ram*. John derided "Yesterday," accused Paul of being just another pretty face, and claimed Paul's music was just elevator Muzak. John knew Paul incredibly well, and said what he knew would hurt the most.

For the title song, "Imagine," John had taken his inspiration from Yoko's short poems in *Grapefruit*. The song was tender, astonishingly simple, and powerful, a testimony to a pure way of seeing the world without boundaries, hunger, possessions, greed, or religion.

John and Yoko were tremendously excited, sure they had created a "New Music," a fusion of avant-garde-jazz-rock and East and West. But John's collaborations with Yoko also had a familiar competitive edge for him. "I sometimes am overawed by her talent," he admitted. "I think, fuck, I better watch out, she is taking over, I better get meself in here." As he had with Paul, John was constantly sizing up their collaborations, making sure he was first.

The mood at Tittenhurst Park was increasingly tense. Yoko was resentful of the ongoing Beatle battles, missing her daughter, tired of the vitriolic press coverage. She and John frequently bickered with each other. It was time to get out of the oppressive atmosphere in England.

Just before they left for America in early September, John and Yoko appeared on a BBC talk show. Yoko read excerpts from *Grapefruit*, which the host admitted he found incomprehensible. His reaction summed up John's trapped feeling in England: Most Brits didn't understand the book, didn't appreciate Yoko, didn't grasp John's new direction. In New York, where the avant-garde flourished, there were people who would appreciate them.

The conversation inevitably turned to the Beatles. John linked the Zen-infused lessons Yoko was teaching him with the Beatles, a life others worshipped but which had become stifling to him: "There's a beautiful story Yoko told me about a Japanese monk. . . . He loved this fantastic golden temple so much that he didn't want to see it disintegrate. So he burned it. . . . That is what I did with the Beatles. I never wanted them to slide down, making comebacks."

John was completely, totally, and irrevocably done with being a Beatle, but just who was he? Thirty years old, half of *JohnandYoko,* newly John Winston Ono Lennon, he set off for New York in pursuit of his new identity.

11

SLIPPING AND SLIDING

1971–1975

"Nobody controls me. I'm uncontrollable. The only one
who controls me is me, and that's just barely possible."

USED TO HYSTERICAL mobs materializing whenever he appeared, John ventured anxiously out into the streets. To his surprise, the rush and confusion of New York offered him some anonymity. People hurried by, busy with their own business, only occasionally saying hello or asking him to shake hands. John loved the excitement of the city, the fast, aggressive energy of New Yorkers. "It's bustin' like crazy," he said, "and when you're here you feel it with the result that it either wears you out or you go right along with it."

After a stay at the ritzy St. Regis Hotel on Fifth Avenue, John and Yoko moved into a small apartment at 105 Bank Street in Greenwich Village, well known to Yoko from her earlier years in the avant-garde art scene. The Village was just what John had been craving. Stepping outside his front door, he was in a neighborhood filled with artists, poets, writers, and political activists. He could stroll anywhere he wanted, or flag down a taxi. It was a heady freedom he hadn't had in years.

Bob Dylan showed up and took John on a walking tour of his favorite parts of the Village.

At home in their new apartment on Bank Street in Greenwich Village, New York, 1972.

Abbie Hoffman and Jerry Rubin, who'd started the radical Youth International Party (YIPPIE), sought out John and Yoko the minute they arrived. John was nervous about getting together with them. He thought to himself, "Be careful, bomb-throwing freaks." He found Hoffman and Rubin were not like they'd been portrayed in the media, but had a strategy similar to John and Yoko's: The more visual and surreal their "protest," the more media attention they'd get. A few years earlier, Hoffman had declared that he would perform an exorcism on the Pentagon and levitate the building. Arrested beforehand while "measuring" the Pentagon, he garnered more publicity by outrageously claiming he was trying to figure out how many witches he'd need to pull off the levitation.

John and Yoko's apartment on Bank Street became *the* place to hang out. The phone rang constantly with people wanting them to participate in benefit concerts, come to meetings, and support their causes. Jerry Rubin was at their apartment often: talking, brainstorming, listening to John sing. "I heard 'Imagine' so many times," Rubin said, "I thought my ears would

Abbie Hoffman talking to a reporter in New York City, September 1969. He and six others, known as the Chicago Seven, had been charged with conspiring to riot at the 1968 Democratic Convention in Chicago.

Jerry Rubin with John and Yoko at a press conference in New York City, around 1971. OVERLEAF: December 1971. John performs his song "John Sinclair" as part of a ten-hour benefit concert for Sinclair, a Michigan counterculture leader.

fall off." People came with all kinds of drugs and offered them to John. Rubin watched him mellow out when he smoked dope, get aggressive on cocaine, and become sad when he dipped back into heroin.

"This was a bitter period for John," said Rubin. "Bitter, bitter, bitter. He was bitter about Paul McCartney. He ranted and raved about Paul. . . . Ranted and raved about being a celebrity. He hated it."

As part of his new, post-Beatle, politically aware state, John spoke out against racism and sexism, saying Yoko had opened his eyes. She pointed out sexism to him right as it was happening to her or other women. For the first time in his life he saw—and was shocked at—how women were subject to continual prejudice. Yoko also deepened his understanding of how racism figured into the Vietnam War. "I just know one thing," John said. "They've never dropped atom bombs or napalm on any whites anywhere."

Caught up in the rush and fervor of left-wing politics, John and Yoko performed in Ann Arbor, Michigan, in defense of John Sinclair, jailed ten years for possession of two joints. They also took part in a benefit concert for victims of the recent uprising at New York's Attica State Prison, where state troopers had killed thirty-two prisoners and ten hostages. John demonstrated with the Onondaga Indians in Syracuse, New York, and showed up at the trial of the Harlem Six, black men who'd been charged with murder and held without bail or a trial.

Besides his political involvement, John was enthusiastic about his new plans for performing music. He didn't want the Plastic Ono Band to be like gods up on the stage, as the Beatles had become. "I just want to be a musician," he said, "and transmit some love back to the people." The Plastic Ono Band would go from town to town, perform with local groups, and donate all the proceeds to the poor and to prisoners.

What John envisioned was thrilling—it would bring together two distinct parts of the political left: The community organizers would promote local issues like environmental cleanup and police brutality, and the media activists like Rubin and Hoffman would grab the headlines on the big issue of the Vietnam War. John's presence was galvanizing. There was a new excitement in the air, a feeling that real change was now just around the corner.

A friend of Rubin's, Stew Alpert, watched John fling himself into left-wing politics. "You wonder, when a person gets so rich and famous, where their motivation comes from," Alpert said. "You're not hungry any more. Politics was a new hunger for John. It was a new world to learn."

In early December 1971, Yoko received news that Tony and Kyoko had resurfaced. A court in Houston, Texas, had granted Tony temporary custody of Kyoko, with Yoko being given visitation rights. Yoko and John flew out on December 18, eager to see Kyoko again. But when they arrived, Tony hid Kyoko with friends and refused to let Yoko and John see her. Even being jailed for five days on contempt of court charges didn't change his mind.

Yoko and John returned to New York devastated. Yoko cried every night, unable even to bear seeing children on television. Tony and Kyoko vanished again, slipping away to California to live underground.

Yoko and John quickly returned to their political work. Wanting to reach middle America, they appeared on David Frost's talk show in January 1972. Besides an informal interview, they sang "Attica State," written earlier for the benefit concert, lamenting the loss of lives and the women made widows by the shoot-out. The audience was less than sympathetic.

John and Yoko weren't deterred by their reception. In mid-February they co-hosted Mike Douglas's talk show, bringing on Jerry Rubin, crusader Ralph Nader, and Black Panther Bobby Seale. John booked Chuck Berry, and they sang two of Berry's hits together, "Memphis" and "Johnny B. Goode." John couldn't believe he was performing with his idol.

John and Chuck Berry rock out together on The Mike Douglas Show *in February 1972. John was in awe of Berry both as a performer and as a songwriter.*

Despite how intimately John understood the insanity and falsehood of rock stardom, Chuck Berry still seemed larger than life. "Chuck Berry is one of the all-time great poets, a rock poet you could call him," John said. "We all owe a lot to him, including Dylan. I've loved everything he's done, ever."

On February 29, 1972, John and Yoko were informed their U.S. visas had expired. They were granted routine extensions to reapply, then suddenly their extensions were revoked. They had ten days to get out of the country. The ostensible reason was that John was unwelcome due to his 1968 drug conviction. The real reason was far more complex.

A few weeks earlier, the FBI had begun an investigation, after Senator Strom Thurmond sent a secret memo to the attorney general reporting that John planned to participate in a national concert tour that would combine politics and rock music and deliver a message urging young people to register to vote, and to vote against the war. Thurmond suggested deportation.

The street violence and the growing political power of the Left frightened President Nixon. He was leading a country torn by racial strife and exhausted by an expensive, bloody, and demoralizing war. Focused on his upcoming reelection, Nixon was ruthless in dealing with any opposition. John, with his loyal fans and impressive ability to get media coverage, was too powerful, far too glamorous, and too charismatic to leave alone.

J. Edgar Hoover, head of the FBI, took the investigation seriously enough to be personally involved. Hoover's efforts to "neutralize" the Left included putting out damaging stories, particularly about sex and money, to the news media. The truth was irrelevant—he wanted to do damage any way he could get away with. John Ehrlichman, counsel to the president, later wrote bluntly about FBI tactics. "The Bureau," he described, "dealt extensively in rumor, gossip and conjure."

Reports were often based on "confidential sources," which could mean illegal wiretapping and bugging, even outright lies. A few months earlier, the Saint Louis *Globe-Democrat* reported John had been seen giving Abbie Hoffman five thousand dollars in cash. The *Globe-Democrat* "sources" reported John wanted some of the money to go to people on the run after planting bombs. The article was a massive lie. John consistently refused to support political violence.

John and Yoko hired a high-profile immigration lawyer, Leon Wildes, to represent them. Wildes laid out a careful strategy with them for their defense. One of his problems was to try to keep John from shooting off his mouth. Wildes turned up more than one hundred foreigners who'd been granted resident status despite having convictions at least as serious as John's. "There are narcotics dealers that've been allowed to stay," John said to the press. "Murderers, rapists, multiple convictions for dope, heroin, cocaine. What the hell. I'll fit right in."

John refused to let the possible deportation stop him from addressing a huge crowd at a national peace rally in New York on April 22, 1972, protesting the bombing of North Vietnam. But he was increasingly nervous.

When he walked out of his apartment, he'd see agents standing across the street, watching him. He'd jump in a taxi and they would follow, with no attempt to remain hidden. John didn't realize it, but he was being "tailgated," a kind of harassment by the FBI intended to make people jumpy and paranoid. John discovered his phone and his lawyer's were tapped. "Suddenly I realized this was serious, they were coming for me, one way or another. They were harassing me."

The fears of John and others were justified. G. Gordon Liddy, working for CREEP, the Committee to Re-Elect the President, considered Communists, liberals, and students alike to be enemies of America. He secretly proposed spending a million dollars on covert activities including beating up protestors, and abducting Jerry Rubin and Abbie Hoffman and taking them to Mexico. The attorney general didn't go for it, but okayed Liddy's subsequent plan to break into the Watergate offices of the Democratic National Committee headquarters to photograph papers and wiretap phones.

The FBI claimed their efforts to deport John were a legitimate enforcement of the law. But John hadn't committed any criminal acts in America: He'd built no bombs, nor had he advocated violent overthrow of the government. Even his conviction for marijuana possesion had been in another country. With the First Amendment right to free speech extending to noncitizens as well as Americans, John had the right to speak out at rallies and sing his protest and peace songs.

Ralph Gleason, a well-known music critic, was appalled at the lack of support for John. "Where the hell is everybody?" he wrote in *Rolling Stone* magazine. "Where are all those who grew up and learned to make music and song turned on by the Beatles? There isn't an artist in the *Billboard* Top 200 albums who shouldn't be picketing the Immigration Office, writing letters in John's defense and campaigning actively to get him off this bum rap." An outpouring of letters flooded Congress.

On June 12, John and Yoko released a new album, *Some Time in New York City*. The album was an explosion of songs about their political work, including one with the highly controversial title "Woman Is the Nigger of the World." John hotly defended it as the first women's liberation song.

On election night, November 1972, John and Yoko joined a group gathered at Rubin's apartment to watch Nixon's landslide reelection to the presidency. John, wall-eyed drunk, disappeared into the bedroom with a woman. The wall was thin, and everyone in the living room could hear the noises they were making. Someone quickly put on a Bob Dylan record. When John finally came out of the room, Yoko had gone completely white.

Rubin urged Yoko to forgive John. He'd been upset and discouraged like everyone else. Besides, he was drunk. But it wasn't that simple for Yoko. She was deeply hurt by John.

In spite of what had happened, John and Yoko wanted to buy their own apartment in Manhattan. Yoko decided she'd like to move into the Dakota, a luxury apartment building on the corner of Central Park West and Seventy-Second Street. She called to ask if anything was available, and was told she'd have to wait two or three years. Twenty minutes later she received a call back—an apartment was available immediately. For Yoko, it was an example of the power of mental telepathy. They moved into an apartment on the seventh floor, with windows overlooking Central Park. Yoko ran their company, Lenono, from the building as well.

At the Dakota, John spent more time in the apartment and less on political activity. For his own reasons, John had been growing increasingly disenchanted with both Rubin and Hoffman. "Count me out if it is for violence," he'd say to them. "Don't expect me to be on the barricades unless it is with flowers." He wasn't sure they could communicate with people, let alone lead them. John's concerns deepened when the FBI spread rumors that Rubin and Hoffman were undercover informants using a technique known as putting on a "snitch jacket." John didn't know what to believe. Not sure who to trust, not knowing if he would even be allowed to stay in America, John's songwriting took a more personal turn.

At a press conference on April 1, 1973, John and Yoko discussed the deportation order with the media. Suddenly they pulled handkerchiefs out of their pockets and announced the founding of the country of Nutopia, a conceptual country with no boundaries and no passports, just people. The white handkerchiefs were the Nutopia flag. As the ambassadors of Nutopia, they asked for diplomatic immunity.

Wildes was blindsided by their Nutopia event. Yoko later apologized to him, saying they were artists and had a message they had to get out. "It was nice of her to take the time to explain it to me," Wildes said dryly.

In July, John headed back into the studio with a group of top-notch musicians to record *Mind Games*. On the album he included a song of apology to Yoko, "Aisumasen (I'm Sorry)," and the John Cage–inspired "Nutopian International Anthem": a few seconds of silence.

Living and working together twenty-four hours day, pressures between John and Yoko built to the explosive point. Their inability to locate Kyoko, as well as the immigration fight,

John and Yoko announce the founding of Nutopia on April 1, 1973. To the left of John is their lawyer, Leon Wildes.

were constant sore points, financially and emotionally. In the eighteen months since his original deportation order, John's lawyers had filed numerous legal papers, and John had made six court appearances. Yoko discovered she'd already been granted permanent residency when she was married to Tony Cox, but John was under orders to leave the country in sixty days. Wildes, arguing that it would be unfair to force Yoko to choose between Kyoko and John, continued trying to get John permanent residency.

Always volatile and hard to live with, the tension made John especially difficult. Holed up alone in his bedroom, he smoked and drank, often emerging petulant and short-tempered.

In September, Yoko decided she'd had enough. She told him to leave, and suggested he head for Los Angeles. John jumped at the chance. He was floundering in New York, his original enthusiasm turned into an anxious apathy. It wouldn't help Wildes argue his case, but John didn't care. He wanted out.

There was another problem: John wouldn't be able to handle Los Angeles on his own.

John in Los Angeles.

All his life, his most fundamental needs had been provided by others. He didn't know how to go grocery shopping, wash his clothes, or withdraw money from a bank. He'd never driven in America, and found it difficult to make even simple phone calls. Yoko had a solution: their twenty-two-year-old assistant, May Pang. She was incredibly diligent, adored John, and loved his music. May didn't smoke, use drugs, or drink. Yoko suggested May accompany John, then went a step further and encouraged them to become lovers. After all, it was better than having him tumbling in and out of bed with different groupies every night.

At first, John was ecstatic to be in Los Angeles, happy to be with May. They were offered a house to live in by a record producer, Lou Adler. May took care of everything. John was free to sleep the morning away and spend the afternoon reading the newspaper, watching television, or sunbathing by the pool with a book and a pack of cigarettes.

At night John was eager to go out clubbing at the Troubadour, the Roxy, and the Rainbow, drinking and partying till the early hours of the morning. He was introduced to Brandy Alexanders, which quickly became his favorite drink. He ordered doubles and knocked them back like milk shakes. When May protested, he brushed off her concerns.

From New York, Yoko kept careful track of John. She called frequently, wanting to know what he and May were doing, how he was feeling, who he was seeing, where he was going. Sometimes John laughed and joked with her, other times he slammed down the phone in anger. Yoko spoke nearly as often to May, instructing her how to handle John, what to do when the paparazzi caught them together, and what to say to the media. The message to May was clear: Though May loved John, and he told May he loved her, Yoko was in charge of their relationship.

John called Phil Spector, who had produced *Let It Be*, and who lived in Los Angeles, and asked if he would produce an album of John's favorite rock'n'roll songs. At first Spector refused. But when John said he could have control—total control—he agreed to take it on. Both May and Yoko were nervous about John working with Spector. They'd seen Spector could be unpredictable and volatile in the recording studio, his sessions degenerating into pandemonium. John wouldn't listen. He insisted Spector's Wall of Sound was exactly what his rock'n'roll album needed.

In October 1973, they started the recording sessions in high spirits. But it wasn't long before the sessions completely degenerated, turning tense as Spector browbeat the musicians and screamed at anyone who disagreed with him. But the music rolled out. With driving drums, tight guitar, and swinging brass sections, the musicians made a poignant contrast to John's rough-edged, melancholy voice as they recorded classics like "Bony Maronie," "Ain't That a Shame," and "Sweet Little Sixteen."

These were the songs John loved. It was a satisfying full circle back to his pre-Beatle days: He'd been singing another classic, "Be-Bop-a-Lula," the first time he met Paul.

One night as they recorded "Angel Baby," John sat on the sidelines for hours, gulping from a flask of vodka and fuming while Spector worked with the other musicians. He wasn't used to being kept waiting in the studio. By the time John recorded his vocals in the early morning, it was clear he was hysterically drunk.

For many months May Pang hung back when the press photographed John. For this 1974 photograph, he grabbed May and roughly kissed her. The pop singer Harry Nilsson, who introduced John to Brandy Alexanders, is on the right.

Back at the house with May, Spector, and a few of the musicians, John erupted into a drunken rage, breaking furniture, throwing vases against windows, smashing the framed gold records on the wall. Spector tied him to the bed with neckties and left. John broke loose and charged at May. She ran from the house, terrified.

In the morning, John didn't remember a thing. When he saw the damage he'd done, he was horrified and begged May to forgive him. It wasn't the first or the last time he went on a violent, drunken rampage. In the morning he was always contrite and sweet with May, assuring her he loved her and was sorry.

Despite May's loyalty and forgiveness, John felt isolated and cut off in Los Angeles. During his frequent phone calls with Yoko, John told her how miserable he was, saying, "I don't like this. I'm out of control. I'm drinking. I'm getting into trouble, and I'd like to come home, please." Yoko refused. She said he wasn't ready.

At the Troubadour club one night in March, slugging down Brandy Alexanders and not eating, John went into the bathroom and spotted a clean Kotex on the back of the toilet. He came out with it stuck on his forehead, and wore it till it fell off, drinking and carousing with a group of buddies.

He soon made a return visit to the Troubadour to see the Smothers Brothers perform in an effort to relaunch their comedy and music career. When they came on, John began heckling them, shouting insults. It was a frightening déjà vu for John: "The Bring-Back-the-Smothers-Brothers thing is part of the Bring-Back-the Beatles and Dig-up-John-Kennedy things," he said. The more people told him to shut up, the louder he yelled. The club bouncers grabbed John and shoved him out onto Santa Monica Boulevard.

The press gleefully reported both of his Troubadour transgressions, excoriating him as a foulmouthed drunk. John, reading the accounts in the paper, was embarrassed and angry. He couldn't understand why they were attacking him.

The papers carried the stories all the way back in New York. Yoko called to say she thought wearing the Kotex on his forehead was a pretty good event. It reminded her of when she'd sent him the broken red cup in the box of Kotex. John exhaled in relief.

But he'd had enough of L.A. Just because Yoko didn't want him back didn't mean he couldn't live in New York. He and May flew back in April and moved into the Pierre Hotel on Fifth Avenue. In July, they rented a small apartment on East Fifty-Second Street.

Though he hadn't been able to come up with any new material for several months, being back in New York rejuvenated him. He immediately began writing again, and returned to the studio to record *Walls and Bridges*.

While John was working on the album, eleven-year-old Julian flew over from England for a visit. In the evenings John took Julian with him to the studio. Julian watched John

Disney World, 1974: May Pang encouraged John to have more contact with his son, and arranged for Julian to come to America to visit twice in 1974.

recording, and sat beside his father as he worked the control board. When John sang and played the guitar for his song "Ya Ya," he had the engineers record Julian accompanying him on the snare drum.

John also invited Elton John, whom he admired for both his music and his flamboyant style, to play keyboard on "Whatever Gets You Thru the Night." Elton John thought the song was fantastic. He swore it would be a number one hit. John just laughed. Unlike the Beatles recordings, his solo records didn't fly up to number one. He promised Elton John that if "Whatever Gets You Thru the Night" hit the top of the charts, he'd appear onstage with him.

To John's surprise, "Whatever Gets You Thru the Night" did make number one, and

he appeared with Elton John on Thanksgiving Day, November 28, 1974, at Madison Square Garden. Twenty thousand fans erupted into screams and shouts when John came onto the stage. "I thought what is *this*?" John said. "I hadn't heard it since the Beatles. The place was really rocking."

He sang his new hit and "Lucy in the Sky with Diamonds." His third and last song was one of Paul's, "I Saw Her Standing There." The audience brought the house down, clapping, shouting, stomping, and whistling.

Out in the darkness of the arena, Yoko watched his performance. As John bowed in the middle of all the thunderous noise, she was suddenly struck by how lonely and vulnerable he looked. She began to cry. Someone next to her asked why she was crying. "I'm not crying," she said brusquely. At the end of the show she went backstage to congratulate him.

They began seeing each other, and in late January John abruptly left May and returned to Yoko. He desperately needed her iron will, the uncompromising force of her personality. "I literally could not survive without her," he said.

John performing with Elton John at Madison Square Garden in New York City on Thanksgiving Day, 1974. It was his last live performance.

12

HOUSEHUSBAND IN SEARCH OF HIMSELF
1975-1980

"All those years of trying to be tough and the heavy rocker and heavy womanizer and heavy drinker were killing me. And it is a relief not to have to do it."

JOHN SLIPPED BACK into the Dakota with a sense of reprieve. Here with Yoko, he could manage his feelings of loneliness and alienation. She was edgy enough to take him where he wanted to go, but controlling enough to bring him back, not let him go too far. As a Beatle, he'd smashed through the ego destruction of the sixties, then with Yoko close by his side, he'd reinvented himself as a solo performer, activist, and rock-guru. The last eighteen months had been insane. "Jesus, I had to get away from that," John said, "because somebody was going to die."

Yoko understood as well as John that what he needed now was time away from the music world, a life without the fans who offered him everything, and yet, paradoxically, could give him nothing. The thin, brittle shell John had always worn as protection had finally failed him. He needed time, he said, to breathe. It wasn't easy for John and Yoko to get back in sync. "We realized that there was a lot of—as we call it—holes in our aura," John said, "space that had to be gently healed between us." They rarely went out or had friends over, but spent

---

John photographed at the Dakota on December 8, 1980.

their time together in the apartment. Just weeks after John moved back in, Yoko got pregnant. They were both jubilant, sure the pregnancy was a sign their getting back together was blessed.

John made one of his instantaneous decisions and decided to devote himself to ensuring the pregnancy went well. He anxiously watched every move Yoko made, both of them worried she'd have another miscarriage. Devouring stacks of books on pregnancy and natural childbirth, he insisted Yoko rest in bed in the morning and had one of their assistants run out for freshly made chocolate cake or anything else she craved. Despite their concern, the pregnancy went well, and Yoko was able to spend her days conducting business in her office on the first floor of the Dakota.

On April 30, 1975, the last American marines left Vietnam and the Viet Cong took over. Antiwar protestors across the United States were jubilant. On Mother's Day, May 11, a huge crowd gathered in Central Park for a celebratory "War Is Over" concert. Many musicians performed for free, including Paul Simon, Patti Smith, Richie Havens, and Joan Baez. Despite John and Yoko's involvement in the Peace movement, they didn't attend.

When John wasn't fussing over Yoko, he would nervously swoop down on the piano or pick up a guitar and pluck out a few chords. Since his days in the Quarry Men he'd been pushing himself, running ahead of the pack, taking on the world. Once Beatlemania hit, hundreds of journalists and cameramen had been constantly clamoring for John's attention: his music, his opinion, his latest happening. Long ago his sense of self had become rooted in the John Lennon he saw reflected back in the public eye. He couldn't help agonizing: Just who *was* he if he wasn't playing music, and making headlines in music magazines like *Billboard* and *Rolling Stone*? "I'd go through these periods of panic," John said, "because I was not in the *Billboard* or being seen at Studio 54 with Mick and Bianca. I mean, I didn't exist anymore."

John retreated into their small bedroom. His guitar hung on the wall over the bed, and on a bookcase beside him were his Scott amplifier, books, magazines, a pair of headphones, and the cable control box for the TV. An ashtray and a pack of Gitanes were never out of reach. John spent days lying on his bed, dreaming, reading, watching television, calling Yoko down in the office, asking her what she was doing, when she would be back on the seventh floor.

Yoko and the extensive staff formed a living wall between John and the outside world. Few people could get through to him. Paul, however, refused to give up. Whenever he passed through New York, he'd nervously call, but John was often scathing to him. "You're all pizza and fairy tales," John spat at him once.

Paul was an uncomfortable reminder of John's days as a Beatle. "Mentally," he said, "I was still carrying them around in the back, back, back of my head." Later, John took another call from Paul, picking up the phone and saying, "Yeah? Yeah? Whadda you want?" John sounded so tough and American, Paul snapped back, "Oh, fuck off, Kojak," and slammed down the phone.

One thing John couldn't run from was his immigration battle. His lawyer, Wildes, continued to aggressively push his case through the courts. On October 7, with the baby due any day, Chief Judge Kaufman at the Court of Appeals ruled the courts could not deny John permanent residency due to his marijuana conviction. Judge Kaufman also issued a stern warning, based on the papers that were coming to light, that the courts could not condone "selective deportation based upon secret political grounds." He sent the case back to the Immigration Service. John was stunned: Did this mean that they'd won? Wildes cautiously told John it didn't quite mean he'd won—not yet. But for the first time, things were looking good.

Two days later, on John's thirty-fifth birthday, October 9, 1975, Yoko gave birth by Cesarean section to a baby boy, Sean Taro Ono Lennon. The procedure was complicated, prolonged by a wait for delivery of blood matching Yoko's in case she needed a transfusion. Afterwards Yoko began shaking all over. John held tight to her and yelled to the nurse to go for the doctor. Sean, suffering from mild spasms, was rushed to the pediatric intensive care unit. With both mother and baby having problems, the doctor tested Yoko's urine for drugs.

The test came back positive. John shouted that they hadn't been on drugs, they'd been on a health-food diet. He threatened to take Sean and leave the hospital. The doctor warned John he'd get a court order declaring them unfit parents and take the baby away. They stayed put, Yoko recovering from surgery, Sean hooked up to monitors and tubes in intensive care, John frantic with worry.

As soon as it was clear Yoko and Sean weren't in danger, John called Mimi. Despite his fear, John was ecstatic as he told her about their new son. "He'll be raised internationally," he said, "and he'll be a citizen of the *world*!" John and Yoko were thrilled with the date of Sean's birth: Yoko believed a child born on his father's birthday would inherit his soul.

Several days later, the doctor realized that the drugs in Yoko's urine had come from the medications they'd given her during the Cesarean section, and released Sean, despite his continuing tremors. John and Yoko literally ran from the hospital with their baby. They took turns staying up at night, praying and rubbing Sean with Chinese herbal salve every two hours. Though the tremors cleared up after several months, John continued to feel vulnerable and protective, afraid the authorities could still swoop down on them and take Sean away.

Paul, now the father of three children himself, was allowed to visit, but John wouldn't let him hold Sean. It upset Paul. "You know he wouldn't let me even touch his baby," Paul said later. "He got really crazy with jealousy at times."

Paul and Linda with their children in the mid-1970s. From left: Stella, Mary, and Heather.

When Sean was a few months old, Yoko hired a live-in nanny and told John that since she'd carried the baby for nine months, it was now his turn to be responsible for him. She headed back to her first-floor office. The role switch worked perfectly for both of them.

Responsible for managing John's extensive finances, Yoko decided to embrace their wealth. As an avant-garde artist, she'd always rebelled against her mother's love of luxury. "I felt I never wanted to lead a life like that, thinking so much about gold and diamonds and beautiful clothes." But now, she meditated on the positive aspects of money, visualizing art, diamonds, and silk with love. To help her make financial decisions, she hired psychics, tarot readers, and astrologers. More usefully, she had her father's banking skills: She was a savvy investor and determined negotiator.

She did little of her own artwork. Instead she concentrated on investing, and on dealing with the lawyers handling the old Beatle entanglements. "They're all male," John explained, "just big and fat, vodka lunch, shouting males, like trained dogs, trained to attack all the time." Yoko liked sparring with them, outsmarting them, and winning.

John put word out that he was now a househusband and his days revolved around his son. Critics were quick to point out that he had a lot more help than the average mother, but John retorted he was putting his body where his mouth had been as a feminist.

Four months after Sean's birth, John's recording contract expired. He decided not to renew it. For the first time in fifteen years, he didn't have a contract hanging over his head, pushing him to put out more music.

On July 27, 1976, when Sean was nine months old, another piece of John's freedom fell into place when his long-awaited residency came through. The grinding legal battle was finally over. He could stay in America, and now that he was a resident, he could leave the country and be assured he'd be allowed back in.

John began taking Japanese lessons, and in June 1977 John, Yoko, and Sean, with an entourage of assistants, took a four-month trip to Japan where they settled into the presidential suite at the Hotel Okura. Asked what they were going to do in Japan, John replied, "We're just gonna be, we're just gonna *be*."

Despite an ardent following of fans, John was rarely recognized in Japan. He was able to eat in restaurants, take Sean for bike rides, and visit Japanese baths and Buddhist temples. They spent time with Yoko's family, and, as always, Yoko conducted business by phone. As much as he enjoyed Japan, John was ready to leave before Yoko. He wanted to be back in his own bedroom with his guitar, his amp, and his books by his side, the thrum of New York City just outside the windows. He waited for Yoko to decide the time was right for them to return. By this point, John had total faith in Yoko and allowed her to make all decisions regarding their lives. When a friend asked about it, John replied, "She will say things you will not understand. Go with it. She's always right." Though many people were shocked—even dismayed—that John would leave everything up to Yoko, there was a freedom in never having to consider, never having to be responsible.

Back at the Dakota, John supervised Sean's meals, determined his son would have a healthy diet. Sometimes John took Sean to the Y for swimming lessons, or drew whimsical pen-and-ink drawings of people and animals for him. He learned to bake bread, and was so excited he offered it to the staff and all the delivery boys and drivers who were in and out of the Dakota. His excited feelings quickly disappeared when he saw how fast the bread was eaten, and he quit baking. "Screw this for a lark," he decided. "I don't get a gold record or a knighthood . . . nothing!"

In his new, clean life, John was against putting chemicals in his body, and no longer took LSD, although several times a year he tripped on more natural alternatives—psychedelic mushrooms and peyote. He knew cigarettes were unhealthy, but unable to quit, he took refuge in the theory that his macrobiotic diet would protect him against cancer.

The press, always eager for his attention, kept trying unsuccessfully to get him to grant interviews, make an appearance, do *something* public. His tenacious refusal only made his legend grow. But the neighborhood residents left him alone, proud to consider him one of their own. "It's so safe here," said John. "I feel free walking the streets. Nobody hassles you."

In the evening, John sometimes gave Sean his bath, and they'd lie on the bed watching TV together, wrestling and chatting, then John would kiss Sean good night and hand him over to the nanny to put to sleep.

Despite all the pressures he'd shoved aside, John's moods were still mercurial. In a bad mood, he'd snap and be surly, even with Sean. But John noticed that if he were in one of his prolonged funks, Sean would pick up on it, slam his finger in a door or get a cold. It was a new awareness for John. He had always indulged in his low moods, considering them part of an artist's birthright. For Sean's sake, John tried to change.

John and Yoko outside the Dakota with Sean around 1977.

John and Sean in 1980.

One day he decided to write a song expressing his love for Sean. He tried, but nothing happened. As soon as he quit trying, the lyrics and melody of a song came to him all at once: part lullaby, part prayer for Sean's safety, part pleasure in watching Sean grow. And transcending the rest of the lyrics, the kind of distilled philosophy that John was so amazing at: "Life is what happens to you while you're busy making other plans." When it was done, he put aside his song, "Beautiful Boy (Darling Boy)," without any immediate plans for it.

With more time away from the hectic Beatles years, John reflected back on his time with them in a softer light. "When I slagged off the Beatle thing, it was like divorce pangs, and, me being me, it was blast this, fuck the past," he said. "Why haven't I ever considered the good times instead of moaning about what we had to go through?"

Despite how John had treated him earlier, Paul continued to come by when he was in New York. He quit talking about business, realizing it just brought up the animosity of their breakup. Instead, he stuck to safe subjects. He and John would

Several afternoons a week, John wandered over to Café la Fortuna, a small Italian coffeehouse on West Seventy-First Street. He'd order a cappuccino, smoke, and read the paper.

talk about their kids, or reminisce about Liverpool and Hamburg. Sometimes they just hung out and watched television together.

One night they caught a running joke on the television show *Saturday Night Live*. The producer, Lorne Michaels, had come on to offer the Beatles $3,000 to reunite on *Saturday Night Live*, a dig at the ludicrously high offers that were being reported in the *New York Times*. In fact, Michaels decided, he'd up it to $3,200—$800 apiece! Watching in the Dakota, John turned to Paul, a bit of his old deviltry at work. The show was being filmed live in a

On November 20, 1976, George Harrison (left) and Paul Simon (right) appeared with producer Lorne Michaels on Saturday Night Live, seven months after Michaels's offer of $3,000 for the Beatles to reunite on his show. In his laconic way, George told Michaels he thought the offer was "pretty chintzy."

studio nearby: They could jump in a taxi, show up, and blow everyone's minds. For a crazy minute, they considered it before deciding they were too tired.

But Paul's perseverance paid off: Their old comfortable ways of hanging out with each other had returned. "It was lovely," said Paul simply.

John was opening up in other ways as well. With increasing frequency his irrepressible creativity was bubbling up. He recorded songs on a home tape recorder, accompanying himself on the guitar or piano. He filled several hundred pages with his quirky short stories. He thought that someday, maybe when he was sixty, he'd like to write stories for kids. "I've always had that feeling of giving what *Wind in the Willows* and *Alice in Wonderland* and *Treasure Island* gave to me at age seven and eight. The books that really opened my whole being."

In June 1980, Yoko suggested John sail down to Bermuda on his ocean-going yacht, the *Megan Jaye*. With a seasoned crew, John set off on June fourth. Surrounded only by the endless ocean and sky, he was utterly free. Even the stormy weather was exhilarating. In Bermuda, he was joined by his assistant, as well as Sean and his nanny. The four of them rented a villa on the edge of the water, while Yoko stayed in New York, intent on some business dealings.

John and Sean went swimming and sailing and toured the local botanical garden, where John's eye was caught by a delicate orchid with the interesting name of "Double Fantasy." At night, John went out club hopping. For the first time, he heard "Rock Lobster" by the B-52's. He was amazed how much singer Kate Pearson's shrill shrieks sounded like Yoko. He said to himself, "It's time to get out the old axe and wake the wife up!"

Refreshed and excited, John leapt into songwriting. Whenever he had a new song, or even a few good lyrics and a melody, he called Yoko and sang it to her. Yoko worked on her own songs, singing them back to him. In a

At the piano in the apartment in the Dakota, 1980.

few weeks they had several dozen songs. John was delighted by his rejuvenation. "Here we are," he said in astonishment. "I'm going to be forty, Sean's going to be five. Isn't it *great*! We survived!"

On August 4, 1980, within a week of returning to New York, he and Yoko began recording their songs at the Hit Factory on West Forty-Eighth Street. Yoko set up a room to rest in between takes. Carpets covered the floor; rare orchids and freesias stood in vases. Fresh sushi, sashimi, and teriyaki chicken were brought in daily, and shiatsu masseuses were on call whenever someone needed a massage. Many of the songs were love songs, and Yoko wanted to create just the right ambiance for recording. They taped a large photo of Sean on the wall of the studio where John could see his son as he recorded "Beautiful Boy."

Recording Double Fantasy *at the Hit Factory in New York City, 1980.*

Naming the album *Double Fantasy* after the orchid John had seen, they decided the first track would be "(Just Like) Starting Over." They began the song by ringing Yoko's wishing bell. John used the bell intentionally, harking back to "Mother" on the *John Lennon/Plastic Ono Band* album, with its mournful church bell. "It's taken a long time," John said, "to get from a slow church death bell to this sweet little wishing bell. And that's the connection. To me, my work is one piece."

Double Fantasy was released on November 17, 1980. To publicize the album, John and Yoko stepped back into the spotlight for the first time in years, granting interviews with journalists they trusted. Why now, wondered his fans, after such a lengthy silence? "You breathe in and you breathe out," John said. "We breathed in after breathing out for a long time. The *I Ching* calls it sitting still. A lot more can happen when you're not doing anything than when you appear to be doing something."

Right now, John was in gear, breathing in with joy and excitement, delighted to be making music again. He and Yoko barely skipped a beat after finishing *Double Fantasy*. Impatient to record more songs, they returned to the studio.

On Saturday, December 6, John called Aunt Mimi, telling her how well *Double Fantasy* was doing, sharing his new sweeping dreams for the future. They were even considering a world tour, and would bring Sean to meet her at long last. "John," Mimi said in her gruff, loving way, "you're an idealist looking for a lost horizon. You would make a saint cry!"

Two days later, on Monday the eighth, John and Yoko headed for the studio. As they left the Dakota, John signed an album for a fan standing outside the tall iron gates, Mark Chapman. They spent five hours working on Yoko's song, "Walking on Thin Ice." John was ebullient, sure this was going to be Yoko's first number one hit.

Shortly before 11 P.M., their driver brought them back to the Dakota. They pulled up on Seventy-Second Street in front of the gates, and the doorman swung open their car door. John walked toward the stone arch first, followed by Yoko.

Mark Chapman, still standing out front, called John's name, dropped to one knee with a .38 revolver pointed straight at John, and repeatedly squeezed the trigger. Five bullets hit John just as he was turning back to look over his shoulder. He staggered up the steps to the manager's office, gasped, "I'm shot, I'm shot," and fell to the floor.

At 11:07 P.M., doctors in the nearby Roosevelt Hospital emergency room pronounced

John dead. In front of the Dakota, Chapman had dropped his gun and stood quietly waiting to be arrested.

Back at the Dakota hours later, Yoko called Paul at his farm in Scotland, and Aunt Mimi in Dorset. In the morning, she had the unbearable job of explaining to five-year-old Sean what had happened. She took him to where John lay after being shot, and told him John had been killed by a fan who had liked John, but was confused. A court would decide what would happen to him. Sean wanted to know if she meant a tennis court or a basketball court. "John would have been proud of Sean if he had heard this," Yoko said. It was the way they used to talk to each other, like buddies. Later, Sean cried.

A few days later, John's body was cremated. Rather than a funeral, Yoko asked people to join in a silent vigil for ten minutes on Sunday, December 14 at 2 P.M. "John loved and prayed for the human race," Yoko said. "Please pray the same for him. Please remember that he had deep faith and concern for life and, though he has now joined the greater force, he is still with us here."

On Sunday, fans gathered in cities around the world. Many had traveled for days, leaving friends and family, walking away from work, needing to be with others who understood how they felt. More than thirty thousand spilled out onto the street in front of St. George's Hall in Liverpool. New York's Central Park overflowed with 100,000 stunned, desolate people, listening to John's songs coming from speakers. At two o'clock, the music stopped. Complete silence fell over Central Park.

People stood together, wordlessly praying and meditating—disbelieving, angry, and grief-stricken—searching within themselves for some kind of strength of heart. John's murder was incomprehensible, the vulnerability unbearable, the loss inconsolable.

At 2:10, the simple piano chords of "Imagine" came over the speakers. John's voice, reflective and tender, filled the air. As the last violin and piano notes faded away, the crowd slowly began to drift apart.

LEFT: Yoko leaving the Roosevelt Hospital after John was shot, accompanied by a policeman and music producer and friend David Geffen. They didn't realize reporters and photographers were waiting outside the door of the hospital. OVERLEAF: Thousands of fans gathered outside the Dakota after hearing that John had been killed.

AFTERWORD
JOHN'S LEGACY

"What's talent? I don't know. Are you born with it? Do you discover it later on? . . . It's a load of crap that I discovered a talent. I just did it."

IN THE LATE 1970s, George Martin came to visit John at the Dakota. They sat together in the kitchen, "mulling over past glories," Martin said, "like a pair of old codgers." John said if he had the chance, he'd do over everything he'd recorded as a Beatle. Shocked, Martin asked if he'd redo "Strawberry Fields Forever," a song Martin considered a masterpiece. "Especially Strawberry Fields Forever," John said emphatically. "Most of what the Beatles did was rubbish."

George Martin knew John well enough to understand. "For John, the vision was always better than the reality," Martin said. "Everything inside him was greater than its expression in the outside world. That was his life."

Yoko spent the first months after John's death in her darkened room, smoking, eating chocolate cake, inconsolable. Paul and Linda came to visit, and the three of them sat and talked, overwhelmed with tears. "We all cried so hard, you know, we just had to laugh," said Paul. "The relief was indescribable." John, who'd cracked open the despair of death with laughter so many times himself, would have understood.

John listening to the White Album in his London flat, 1968.

After several months of isolation, Yoko had to decide: Would she go forward, or not? She pulled herself together, reemerging both softened and hardened: more tender and available to Sean, tougher with the outside world.

She continued to run the business, parlaying their money into a fortune, while keeping up her work as an artist. Every year, she released something new of John's—unheard music, drawings, or writing. As an artist herself, she knew he'd want people to know his work.

In 1981, 2.5 acres of Central Park across from the Dakota were named after John's song "Strawberry Fields Forever." On John's birthday, October 9, 1985, Yoko and Sean ceremonially opened Strawberry Fields, and the area was designated a Garden of Peace. A reproduction of a black-and-white mosaic from Pompeii, with the word *Imagine* in the center, was installed in the middle of the wide pathway.

Paul and George expressed their loss in the way they knew best: music. George, at work on an album when John was shot, wrote and recorded "All Those Years Ago" in the spring of 1981. Paul and Ringo joined him in the studio. A few months later, at his farm in Scotland, Paul recorded his tribute, "Here Today."

Fans, always hungry for more, never quit clamoring for a Beatle reunion. Fed up, George finally said in frustration in 1989, "As far as I'm concerned, there won't be a Beatles reunion as long as John Lennon remains dead."

The three of them went on with their separate music careers. Paul's band, Wings, after a wildly successful run of singles, albums, and concerts, broke up. He continued as a solo artist, releasing a number of albums, and worked in other art forms, writing soundtracks and scripts, and exhibiting his paintings.

George, in addition to writing music, recording, and touring, formed his own film company, Handmade Films, in 1978. Feeling the energy and spirit of the Beatles was now in the irreverent humor of the Monty Python group, he produced several of their highly successful films. Ten years later he got together with four other rock'n'roll greats: Roy Orbison, Bob Dylan, Jeff Lynne, and Tom Petty, to form a "super-group," the Traveling Wilburys.

Ringo appeared in several films and made albums, gathering together friends in the

The three remaining Beatles together in 1995.

rock'n'roll community to record with him. He's most beloved for his roles as narrator and Mr. Conductor on *Thomas the Tank Engine and Friends*.

Early in 1994, John was inducted into the Rock'n'Roll Hall of Fame as a solo musician. Shortly afterwards, Yoko gave Paul demo tapes for four songs John had recorded in the late seventies, sitting at his piano with a mono tape recorder. She asked if he and George and Ringo would like to pick two of them and complete them as songs. They chose "Free as a Bird" and "Real Love."

The unimaginable happened: The Beatles were back in the studio, even if John was only on tape. Paul said they should pretend they'd just about finished some recording and then John had gone off on a holiday and asked them to finish up.

Ringo said, "Oh! This could even be joyous!"

"And it was," said Paul. "It actually was."

"Free as a Bird" and "Real Love" were released as singles and as part of an anthology series, each album rushing to the top of the Billboard charts. *Anthology 3* was their third album to hit number one within a year. "The last time that ever happened," said George Martin wryly, "it was achieved by a group called The Beatles."

The success was bittersweet for the remaining Beatles. "The three of us got pretty close again there," said Ringo, "and still there's that empty hole, that *is* John." They knew him like no one else ever could. They'd been four scruffy lads from Liverpool with big dreams, who'd made it very, very big. They'd been on the road together, on stages all over the world, and in the studio when John would rush in with grand plans for the rock'n'roll playing in his head. Other musicians wanted to be heard. That wasn't enough for John. He wanted to be *felt*.

His contradictions were staggering. Tender and vulnerable, he was brash and invincible. Impulsive, headstrong, and defiant, he needed to be contained. Swearing he was fiercely independent, he was utterly dependent on having someone strong—Mimi, Paul, Yoko—to keep him from flying out of orbit. A brilliant, charming spin-doctor, he knew how to manipulate the press, giving them honesty as he saw it, honesty for the moment, not honesty-to-the-bone. He behaved badly, outrageously, ruthlessly, then was contrite and filled with remorse. At least, until the next time.

Both of John's sons chose careers in rock'n'roll, releasing CDs and touring. Their music is compared to John's, dissected for flashes of his inspired lyrics. People scan their faces for a glimpse of John—Sean's jaw line, Julian's hair hanging over his forehead, a familiar mischievous glance from their eyes. But their greatest loss is personal, the father neither knew well, but the world claims as its own. "Sometimes I walk into a store and 'Instant Karma' is playing and I feel like that's him talking to me," said Sean. "I wish I could do anything with my dad. Go to a movie. Walk down the street. Watch TV with him, let alone talk about music."

Their loss held an uncanny echo from John's childhood: At five, Sean was the same age John was when he went from his mother to his aunt Mimi; Teenage Julian lost his father, just as John had irrevocably lost his mother.

In August 1989, Yoko, Julian, Sean, and Cynthia shared time together before Julian performed at a benefit concert held at the Beacon Theater in New York City.

Cynthia tried to put her years with John behind her, and move on with her life. She married several times, but never had any more children. Finally she realized she would always be known for being married to John.

Aunt Mimi never recovered from John's murder. She sold her house overlooking the sea and moved back to Liverpool, where she lived until her death in December 1991.

Mark Chapman, sentenced to twenty years to life, is incarcerated at Attica State Prison, the same prison John and Yoko had memorialized in their song, "Attica State." He's come up for parole several times but been denied.

Yoko's daughter Kyoko called her in 1997, three weeks after giving birth to her own daughter, Emi. Yoko and Kyoko hadn't seen each other in more than twenty-five years. They slowly established a relationship, but it wasn't always easy. Nor has it been easy for Yoko to be both mother and father to Sean. What she loved best was doing her artwork.

"Motherhood is extremely complicated and difficult," she said, "though I suppose some mothers would say it's as natural as breathing."

In 1997 George underwent surgery for throat cancer, candidly admitting it was due to his heavy cigarette smoking. With the cancer in remission, he survived a violent knife attack by a fan who got past his home security system. The cancer reappeared, metastasizing to his lungs and brain, and he died on November 29, 2001. Exactly one year later, rock stars gathered for a tribute performance, "Concert for George." Ravi Shankar composed a song for George, and Billy Preston led Paul, Ringo, Eric Clapton, and others in a bluesy rendition of one of George's most popular songs, "My Sweet Lord." Fans around the world mourned George's passing, and finally accepted that the Beatles would never perform together again.

In an interview with RKO radio network just six hours before his death, John spoke about the opening up that had occurred during the sixties. "The thing the sixties did," he said, "was show us the possibility and responsibility that we all had. It wasn't the answer. It just gave us a glimpse of the possibility."

The possibilities took root and grew. The civil rights movement scored critical victories and created multicultural awareness; the hippie legacy spawned environmental protection, the peace movement, and alternative health care; questioning of social norms led to feminism and gay liberation.

Decades after John's death, the energy of change still resonates in his fierce rock'n'roll anthems like "Revolution," and "Come Together," and in tender, evocative songs like "Imagine," and "Beautiful Boy (Darling Boy)." John and his music are still charismatic, mysterious, and contradictory.

Who was he, really? What inspired him to pull together the elusive filaments of such beautiful music? Perhaps he said it best himself, in a rare moment of honest-to-the-bone. "I want people to love me," John said. "I want to be loved."

Strawberry Fields in Central Park.

SOURCE NOTES

THERE ARE LITERALLY hundreds of books written about John Lennon. They include excellent biographies and well-researched Beatles stories as well as numerous books by people who knew John, loved him, hated him, worked for him (or all of the above). There's a massive amount of nonfiction on rock music, the sixties, and twentieth-century history citing Lennon's contributions. An unfortunate number of books print misinformation, which recycles dizzyingly through other authors' volumes. And slung in with all of these are a few of the most deluded, trashiest books I've ever read, full of wild assumptions and sensational claims presented as facts.

I made my way through this paper-and-print jungle with a machete, and found one of the best sources of information about John was John himself: One way he explored his feelings was to talk to other people about himself. Over the years he developed a number of long-term relationships with journalists and could be astonishingly candid with them. I relied on these direct quotes whenever possible, bearing in mind that John could—and frequently did—change his mind over time, often radically, or stretch the truth to tell a good story. His songs evolved into intensely personal and autobiographical lyrics, and there are hours of film and video and thousands of photographs of him available. By triangulating primary source materials—his view of himself and the views of others close to him—with solidly researched works, a revealing, multidimensional picture of John emerged. It wasn't necessary for me to speculate how John felt: Either he said how he was feeling, or a reliable source close to him revealed his actions, shared thoughts, and feelings.

Separating John-the-person from John-the-myth presented its own challenge. Rumors and myths about all the Beatles grew as quickly as their fame. Often a story about one of the Beatles' lives is just that—a story based on a kernel of truth that's become blown out of proportion or mythologized. I've done my best to find my way back to what actually happened, to who John really was.

In phone calls and e-mails, several people who knew John as a child were helpful to me. Regrettably, I had little contact with other people who were close to John during his life. But many of them, including Pete Shotton, Julia Baird, Paul McCartney, George Martin, Cynthia Lennon, and May Pang, have spoken or written extensively about John and their relationships with him.

A number of good books are particularly informative about specific periods of John's life, and others stand out for their broad, well-researched scope. They can be found in the Further Reading List following the bibliography.

Introduction

"In me secret heart . . .": Wenner, *Lennon Remembers*, 93.

"These guys were sweating . . ." "Because we'd been . . ." and "protest against . . .": Wiener, *Come Together: John Lennon in His Time*, 88.

"It's part of our policy . . .": Wiener, *Come Together*, 91.

"Peace, brother" and "Youth is the future . . .": Coleman, *Lennon*, 400.

"the United States . . .": Kurlansky, *1968: The Year That Rocked the World*, xviii.

"All I'm saying . . .": Coleman, *Lennon*, 397.

"Give it a *chance*.": Coleman, *Lennon*, 400.

"forever, and not stopping . . .": Wiener, *Come Together*, 97.

Chapter One

"It's that same problem . . .": Sheff and Golson, *The Playboy Interviews*, 133.

"Oh, be quiet" "It's a boy . . ." and "I'll never forget . . .": Norman, *Shout!*, 4.

"bug-ridden, lice ridden . . .": www.liverpoolpictorial.co.uk/bessiebraddock/

"Got any gum . . ." and John's cousin Stanley . . . : phone interview with Stanley Parkes, April 12, 2005.

"That's enough . . .": Coleman, *Lennon*, 22.

"Well—you couldn't . . .": Norman, *Shout!*, 7.

"Dear George . . .": Davies, *The Beatles*, 9.

"George, you're ruining . . .": Coleman, *Lennon*, 27.

"His mind . . .": Solt and Egan, *Imagine: John Lennon*, 20.

"And when he said . . .": Coleman, *Lennon*, 23.

"It was like . . ." and "My feeling never died . . .": Davies, *The Beatles*, 12.

"Excuse my dirty . . ." and "Come in . . .": Sellers, Secombe, and Milligan, *The Goon Show*, "Napoleon's Piano" episode.

"'Twas brillig . . .": Lewis Carroll, *Through the Looking Glass*.

"I used to *live* . . .": Davies, *The Beatles*, 10.

"Listen you . . ." and "Winnie, Winnie, Winnie . . .": Shotton and Schaffner, *John Lennon in My Life*, 21.

"A penis is . . .": Davies, *The Quarrymen*, 249.

"I just see and hear *differently* . . .": Sheff and Golson, *The Playboy Interviews*, 134.

"I've just seen . . .": Coleman, *Lennon*, 39.

"happy as the day . . .": Davies, *The Beatles*, 12.

"I was always seeing . . .": Sheff and Golson, *The Playboy Interviews*, 133–34.

"Christ": Davies, *The Beatles*, 13.

Chapter Two

"Rock'n'roll was real . . .": *The Beatles Anthology* (Apple Corps, 2003), episode 1.

"I wanted to be . . .": Davies, *The Beatles*, 13.

"If you think . . .": Shotton and Schaffner, *John Lennon in My Life*, 32.

"Snowball": Shotton and Schaffner, *John Lennon in My Life*, 21.

"What's that . . .": Davies, *The Beatles*, 14.

"I think the roof's . . .": Shotton and Schaffner, *John Lennon in My Life*, 32.

"Our late editor . . .": Henke, *Lennon Legend*, 8.

"I do": Coleman, *Lennon*, 48.

Though he rarely…: Sheff and Golson, *The Playboy Interviews*, 132.

"I would find . . ." "The only contact . . ." and "Surrealism had a . . .": Sheff and Golson, *The Playboy Interviews*, 134.

"The sort of gang . . .": Davies, *The Beatles*, 11.

"John was always . . .": Norman, *Shout!*, 9.

"John used to look . . .": Norman, *Shout!*, 10.

"We just laughed . . .": Baird with Giuliano, *John Lennon: My Brother*, 28–29.

"She was very strait-laced": *The Beatles: A Long and Winding Road*, Episode One.

"a futuristic paradise . . .": Shotton and Schaffner, *John Lennon in My Life*, 48.

To his immense . . . : Baird with Giuliano, *John Lennon: My Brother*, 42.

"He is so fond . . ." "Still lazy" and "He is certainly . . .": Henke, *Lennon Legend*, 8.

"I wanted something . . .": Halberstam, *The Fifties*, 470.

"I knew that . . ." and "If I could . . .": Halberstam, *The Fifties*, 471.

"What the hell . . .": Halberstam, *The Fifties*, 459.

"After that . . .": Coleman, *Lennon*, 54.

John joined hundreds . . . : Baird with Giuliano, *John Lennon: My Brother*, 42.

"It was Elvis . . .": Coleman, *Lennon*, 55.

John couldn't care less . . .": Shotton and Schaffner, *John Lennon in My Life*, 48.

"You ought to . . .": Coleman, *Lennon*, 42–43.

"Well, it's lovely . . .": Shotton and Schaffner, *John Lennon in My Life*, 37.

"Is this the one . . .": E-mail from Julia Baird, April 6, 2005.

"Better than Elvis . . .": E-mail from Michael Hill, March 15, 2005.

"Both of us . . .": Shotton and Schaffner, *John Lennon in My Life*, 49.

"so great . . .": Hertsgaard, *A Day in the Life*, 19.

For the next year . . . : E-mail from Michael Hill, March 15, 2005.

"Salmon fishing . . .": Harry, *The John Lennon Encyclopedia*, 723.

SOURCE NOTES

"That'll Be the Day": Davies, *The Beatles*, 20.

"We're going to . . .": Coleman, *Lennon*, 55.

Lonnie Donegan's . . . :

news.bbc.co.uk/1hi/entertainment/music/1973037.stm

Chapter Three

"It went through . . .": Davies, *The Beatles*, 33.

She taught them . . .: Baird with Giuliano, *John Lennon: My Brother*, 44.

"First": Coleman, *Lennon*, 60.

"Quarry Men . . .": Shotton and Schaffner, *John Lennon in My Life*, 53.

"Surely you don't . . .": *The Beatles: A Long and Winding Road*, Episode 1.

"Let me get it . . ." and "The guitar's all. .": Coleman, *Lennon*, 63.

"This boy's got . . .": Norman, *Shout!*, 39.

"What are *you* . . .": Davies, *The Beatles*, 17.

"Mimi's coming . . .": Norman, *Shout!*, 35.

"Come go with . . .": Miles, *Paul McCartney*, 26.

"I half thought . . .": Davies, *The Beatles*, 33.

Tingles ran up . . . Miles, *Paul McCartney*, 19.

"They must have . . .": Miles, *Paul McCartney*, 20.

"Every time . . .": Davies, *The Beatles*, 30.

"A povre wydwe . . ." and "Dark was the . . .": Miles, *Paul McCartney*, 41.

"There was a . . .": Miles, *Paul McCartney*, 43.

"I really fancied . . .": Miles, *Paul McCartney*, 42.

"I was called . . .": Davies, *The Beatles*, 25.

"I told . . .": Davies, *The Beatles*, 31.

On Friday . . .: Lewisohn, *The Complete Beatles Chronicle*, 15.

Chapter Four

"It was awful . . .": Giuliano, *Two of Us*, 6.

"When I talk . . .": Norman, *Shout!*, 41.

"How can you . . .": Giuliano, *Two of Us*, 6.

"When John came . . .": Coleman, *Lennon*, 87.

"John, your little . . ." and "She was the . . .": Miles, *Paul McCartney*, 44.

Paul wanted it.: Miles, *Paul McCartney*, 45–46.

"It was too . . .": Davies, *The Beatles*, 44.

"George looked even . . .": Davies, *The Beatles*, 45.

"I was just . . .": Davies, *The Beatles*, 39.

"Now there were . . .": Davies, *The Beatles*, 45.

"Knee-trembler": Miles, *Paul McCartney*, 29.

Mimi had gotten . . .: Shotton and Schaffner, *John Lennon in My Life*, 38.

"You must bring . . .": Baird with Giuliano, *John Lennon: My Brother*, 55.

"Being John . . .": Miles, *Paul McCartney*, 48.

He felt frozen . . . : Giuliano, *Two of Us*, 6.

Mimi was beside . . . : Norman, *Shout!*, 50.

"Creepy Jewboy . . .": Shotton and Schaffner, *John Lennon in My Life*, 61.

He'd leer . . . : Coleman, *Lennon*, 96.

"Now we were . . .": Miles, *Paul McCartney*, 49.

"What did he . . .": and John wasn't looking . . . : Miles, *Paul McCartney*, 46.

Chapter Five

"I was raised . . .": Solt and Egan, *Imagine: John Lennon*, 31.

"I looked up . . .": Davies, *The Beatles*, 111.

"No dirty jokes . . .": Norman, *Shout!*, 51.

She was sure . . . : Coleman, *Lennon*, 13.

"I was triumphant . . .": Davies, *The Beatles*, 52.

"I love you . . .": Coleman, *Lennon*, 105.

"He was so . . .": Davies, *The Beatles*, 52.

"I was in a sort . . .": and "Molly, the cleaning . . .": Davies, *The Beatles*, 53.

"Ever since . . .": Laslo Benedek, director, *The Wild One*, screenplay by Ben Maddow and John Paxton, 1958.

"Fuck me . . .": Miles, *Paul McCartney*, 53.

"We were terrible . . .": Davies, *The Beatles*, 66.

"Yeh! You're in . . .": Best and Doncaster, *Beatle!*, 29.

"You're nuts . . .": Best and Doncaster, *Beatle!*, 33.

"Tutti Frutti . . .": Sutcliffe with Thompson, *The Beatles' Shadow*, 92.

"The waiters would . . .": Davies, *The Beatles*, 81.

"Mach Schau! . . .": Miles, *Paul McCartney*, 59.

"We used to . . .": *The Beatles Anthology*, episode 1.

"beknakked Beatles": Best and Doncaster, *Beatle!*, 41.

"German spassies": Best and Doncaster, *Beatle!*, 42.

"I felt ashamed . . .": Davies, *The Beatles*, 89.

"Long Tall Sally": Lewisohn, *The Complete Beatles Chronicle*, 25.

"It was that . . .": Davies, *The Beatles*, 92.

Chapter Six

"I was a hitter . . .": Sheff, "The Playboy Interview," 16.

after a gig . . .: Sutcliffe with Thompson, *The Beatles' Shadow*, 117.

"That John . . .": Coleman, *Lennon*, 137.

"They should have . . .": Davies, *The Beatles*, 100–101.

That left Paul: Davies, *The Beatles*, 371.

"I remember . . .": Davies, *The Beatles*, 108.

"recording stars": Best and Doncaster, *Beatle!*, 149.

"He went into . . .": Coleman, *Lennon*, 162.

"Make up your . . .": Norman, *Shout!*, 161.

"Besame Mucho . . .": Lewisohn, *The Complete Beatles Chronicle*, 70.

"It was like . . .": Davies, *The Beatles*, 153.

"We were cowards . . .": Davies, *The Beatles*, 140.

"Then the really . . .": Davies, *The Beatles*, 151.

"Gentlemen, you've . . .": Martin with Hornsby, *All You Need Is Ears*, 130.

"Oh he's beautiful . . .": Coleman, *Lennon*, 172.

"Who's going to . . .": Lennon, *A Twist of Lennon*, 87.

He introduced Brian . . . and "Don't ever throw . . .": Wenner, *Lennon Remembers*, 63.

"It was almost . . .": Sheff, "The Playboy Interview," 13.

"Spanish honeymoon": Shotton and Schaffner, *John Lennon in My Life*, 74.

"I smashed him . . .": Davies, *The Beatles*, 177.

"What have I done?": Shotton and Schaffner, *John Lennon in My Life*, 74.

Chapter Seven

"It was like . . .": Solt and Egan, *Imagine: John Lennon*, 63.

"We looked at . . .": Miles, *Paul McCartney*, 120.

"I just want . . .": *The Beatles Anthology*, episode 2.

"Will the people . . .": Hertsgaard, *A Day in the Life,* 90.

"A room and . . .": Coleman, *Lennon*, 232.

"Lyrics didn't really . . .": Sheff and Golson, *The Playboy Interviews*, 118.

"Oh you-u . . .": Sheff and Golson, *The Playboy Interviews*, 117.

"He provided . . .": Sheff, "The Playboy Interview," 5.

"We used to . . .": Miles, *Paul McCartney*, 92.

"He must be . . .": Norman, *Shout!*, 214.

"Are those wigs . . .": Norman, *Shout!*, 212.

"tramp smoking . . .": Miles, *Paul McCartney,* 188.

"Cripples, Neil": Davies, *The Beatles*. 176.

It became a secret . . . : Martin with Hornsby, *All You Need Is Ears*, 165.

"Of course . . .": Hertsgaard, *A Day in the Life*, 92–93.

"Queer Jew": Norman, *Shout!*, 287.

"It's like we're . . .": Coleman, *Lennon*, 213.

"Beatles concerts . . .": Coleman, *Lennon*, 214.

thirty-one shows . . . : Phone interview with Mark Naboshek, May 9, 2005.

"He'd just come . . .": Coleman, *Lennon*, 219.

"Before the pill . . .": Miles, *Paul McCartney*, 119.

John, asked if . . . : Lennon, *A Twist of Lennon*, 98.

"I was fat . . .": Sheff and Golson, *The Playboy Interviews*, 150.

"He was in . . .": Coleman, *Lennon*, 304.

"I don't know . . .": Coleman, *Lennon*, 225.

"When we actually . . .": Hertsgaard, *A Day in the Life*, 142–43.

"It was like . . .": Hertsgaard, *A Day in the Life*, 143.

"fucking howl . . .": Wenner, *Lennon Remembers*, 21.

"They were doing . . .": Marcus, "The Beatles," in *The Rolling Stone Illustrated History of Rock and Roll*, 212.

Chapter Eight

"I've always . . .": Wenner, *Lennon Remembers*, 57.

"It just happens . . .": Wenner, "Lennon Remembers," in *The Ballad of John and Yoko*, 102.

In America . . . : Lewisohn, *The Complete Beatles Chronicle*, 351.

"I was . . .": Norman, *Shout!*, 294.

"Up till then . . .": Sheff and Golson, *The Playboy Interviews*, 151.

"So letting it . . .": Sheff and Golson, *The Playboy Interviews*, 163.

"We were just . . .": Wenner, *Lennon Remembers*, 49.

She was miserable . . . : Coleman, *Lennon*, 323.

"I know what . . .": Sheff and Golson, *The Playboy Interviews*, 152.

"Christianity will go . . .": London *Evening Standard*, March 4, 1966.

"I thought they'd . . .": Wiener, *Come Together*, 13.

"I never meant . . .": Coleman, *Lennon*, 316.

members of Prince George's . . . : Lewisohn, *The Complete Beatles Chronicle*, 213.

"obstruction of the . . .": Wiener, *Come Together*, 18.

"We think of . . .": Wiener, *Come Together*, 17.

"The continual awareness . . ." and "I burst out . . .": Wiener, *Come Together*, 21.

"Nice working . . .": Clayson, *George Harrison*, 200.

After more than . . . : Lewisohn, *The Complete Beatles Chronicle*, 214.

"happening" and "member of . . .": Coleman, *Lennon*, 324.

One minute he liked . . . : Wenner, *Lennon Remembers*, 39.

"I do get up . . .": Davies, *The Beatles*, 277.

"I don't like . . ." Miles, *Paul McCartney*, 171.

"We had great . . .": Davies, *The Beatles*, 370.

"It's only me . . .": Davies, *The Beatles*, 373.

"If we could . . .": Miles, *Paul McCartney*, 276.

"That wonderfully . . .": Martin with Pearson, *With a Little Help From My Friends*, 13.

"He expected . . .": Henke, *Lennon Legend*, 20.

In the first . . . : Davies, *The Beatles*, 235.

"I just noticed . . .": Wenner, *Lennon Remembers*, 52.

"I saw paisley . . .": Miles, *Paul McCartney*, 381.

"That was one . . .": Miles, *Paul McCartney*, 209–10.

"Hearing *Sgt. Pepper* . . .": Taylor, *It Was Twenty Years Ago Today*, 165.

"What if you're . . .": Davies, *The Beatles*, 232.

John felt an agonizing . . . : Wenner, *Lennon Remembers*, 63.

"We've fuckin' . . .": Wenner, *Lennon Remembers*, 25.

Chapter Nine

"We are all . . .": Wenner, "Lennon Remembers," in *The Ballad of John and Yoko*, 109.

"Oompah, oompah . . .": Lewisohn, *The Complete Beatles Chronicle*, 268.

"Weirdness is fine . . .": Martin with Pearson, *With a Little Help From My Friends*, 139.

"If I am on . . ." "I can see . . ." and "I have to see . . .": Davies, *The Beatles*, 295.

"When I first . . .": Lennon, *A Twist of Lennon*, 165.

"It's much better . . .": Coleman, *Lennon*, 340.

"It was very . . .": Coleman, *Lennon*, 345.

As a young child . . . : Munro with Hendricks, *Yes Yoko Ono*, 15.

"I had one . . .": Kirk, "In Tokyo," in *The Ballad of John and Yoko*, 22.

"smelling like . . .": Munro with Hendricks, *Yes Yoko Ono*, 13.

"She used to . . .": Kirk, "In Tokyo," in *The Ballad of John and Yoko*, 27.

Her mother also . . . : Coleman, *Lennon*, 425.

"So I just . . .": Cott, "Yoko Ono and Her Sixteen Track Voice," in *The Ballad of John and Yoko*, 116.

"I wanted to throw . . .": Kemp, "She Who Laughs Last," *Music Alternatives*, 78.

She thought constantly . . . : Ono, "My Love, My Struggle," *Bungei Shunju* magazine, 244.

"It was like . . .": Cott, "Yoko Ono and Her Sixteen Track Voice," in *The Ballad of John and Yoko*, 117.

"It was impossible . . .": Hopkins, *Yoko Ono*, 60.

Sure they . . . : Davies, *The Beatles*, 371.

The sessions became . . . : Lewisohn, *The Complete Beatles Chronicle*, 277.

"The critics wouldn't . . .": Lewisohn, *The Complete Beatles Chronicle*, 337.

"It *drove* me out . . .": Sheff and Golson, *The Playboy Interviews*, 163.

"The two of them . . .": Miles, *Paul McCartney*, 567.

"This is the end . . .": Hertsgaard, *A Day in the Life*, 265.

"Once the count-in . . .": *Let It Be Naked*, unpaginated liner notes.

"I was slowly . . .": Wenner, *Lennon Remembers*, 54.

"I got a message . . .": Wenner, *Lennon Remembers*, 53.

"She freed me . . .": Wenner, *Lennon Remembers*, 54.

"I'm starting to . . .": Cott, "Yoko Ono and Her Sixteen Track Voice," in *The Ballad of John and Yoko*, 125.

"It's funky . . .": Sheff and Golson, *The Playboy Interviews*, 170.

Chapter Ten

"I'm not the Beatles . . .": Wenner, *Lennon Remembers*, 134.

"We were just . . .": Shotton and Schaffner, *John Lennon in My Life*, 191.

"When you actually . . .": Solt, *Gimmie Some Truth*, track 4.

"We both sat . . .": Miles, *Paul McCartney*, 530.

"We get into . . .": Miles, *John Lennon in His Own Words*, 78.

"Well, I think . . .": Miles, *Paul McCartney*, 561.

"John's in love . . .": Miles, *Paul McCartney*, 566.

"The sharp-talking . . .": Sheff and Golson, *The Playboy Interviews*, 104.

he felt guilty . . . : Coleman, *Lennon*, 412.

"My thing is . . .": Sheff, "The Playboy Interview," 5.

"We needed . . .": Miles, *John Lennon in His Own Words*, 97.

"We've done . . ." and "I was shattered . . .": Brown and Gaines, *The Love You Make*, 408.

"I sometimes . . .": Cott, "Yoko Ono and Her Sixteen Track Voice," in *The Ballad of John and Yoko*, 115.

"There's a beautiful . . .": Coleman, *Lennon*, 420.

Chapter Eleven

"Nobody controls . . .": Sheff, "The Playboy Interview," 3.

"It's bustin' . . .": Miles, *John Lennon in His Own Words*, 99.

"Be careful . . .": Wiener, *Come Together*, 202.

Hoffman had declared . . . : Taylor, *It Was Twenty Years Ago Today*, 228.

"I heard 'Imagine' . . ." Rubin watched, and "This was a bitter . . .": Wiener, *Come Together*, 178.

"I just know . . .": Wiener, *Come Together*, 186.

"I just want . . .": Werbin, "Some Time in New York City," in *The Ballad of John and Yoko*, 133.

"You wonder . . .": Wiener, *Come Together*, 186.

"Chuck Berry . . .": Wenner, *Lennon Remembers*, 140.

The street violence . . . : White, *Breach of Faith*, 78.

"The Bureau . . ." and illegal wiretapping . . . : Ehrlichman, *Witness to Power*, 158.

The *Globe-Democrat* . . . : Sparkes, St. Louis *Globe-Democrat*, September 30, 1971.

"It was nice . . .": Wiener, *Come Together*, 229.

"There are narcotics . . .": Siegel, "Back in the U.S.S.A.," in *The Ballad of John and Yoko*, 138.

"Suddenly I realized . . .": Coleman, *Lennon*, 478.

He secretly proposed . . . : White, *Breach of Faith*, 157.

"Where the hell . . .": Gleason, "Fair Play for John and Yoko," in *The Ballad of John and Yoko*, 137.

For Yoko . . . : Ono, "My Love, My Struggle," *Bungei Shunju* magazine, 238.

On election night . . . : Lennon, "The Book" in *Anthology* (Capitol Records, 1998), 13.

"Count me out . . .": Sheff, "The Playboy Interview," 16.

"snitch jacket": Wiener, *Come Together*, 230.

John erupted . . . : Pang and Edwards, *Loving John*, 120.

"I don't like . . .": Sheff and Golson, *The Playboy Interviews*, 20.

"The Bring-Back . . .": Sheff and Golson, *The Playboy Interviews*, 23.

He couldn't understand . . . : Sheff and Golson, *The Playboy Interviews*, 22.

John, painfully aware . . . : Coleman, *Lennon*, 499.

"I thought what . . .": Coleman, *Lennon*, 511.

"I'm not crying": Sheff and Golson, *The Playboy Interviews*, 27.

"I literally could . . .": Solt and Egan, *Imagine*, 187.

Chapter Twelve

"All those years . . .": Sheff and Golson, *The Playboy Interviews*, 59.

"Jesus, I had to . . .": Sheff, "The Playboy Interview," 8.

"We realized that . . .": Sheff and Golson, *The Playboy Interviews*, 28.

sure the pregnancy . . . : Coleman, *Lennon*, 518.

"I'd go through . . .": Interview by Jody Denberg, recorded Sept. 7, 2000, New York, Capitol Records, Inc.

"You're all pizza . . .": Miles, *Paul McCartney*, 588.

"Mentally . . .": Sheff and Golson, *The Playboy Interviews*, 41.

"Yeah? Yeah? . . .": Miles, *Paul McCartney*, 588.

"selective deportation . . .": Coleman, *Lennon*, 481. Originally from *The New York Times*, October 8, 1975.

"He'll be raised . . .": Coleman, *Lennon*, 521.

"You know he . . .": Davies, *The Beatles*, 370.

"I felt I never . . .": Coleman, *Lennon*, 526.

"They're all male . . .": Sheff, "The Playboy Interview," 3.

"We're just gonna . . .": Flippo, "The Private Years," in *The Ballad of John and Yoko*, 173.

As much as . . . : Flippo, "The Private Years," in *The Ballad of John and Yoko*, 174.

"She will say . . .": Flippo, "The Private Years," in *The Ballad of John and Yoko*, 168.

"Screw this for . . .": Coleman, *Lennon*, 532.

psychedelic mushrooms . . . : Sheff and Golson, *The Playboy Interviews*, 93.

"It's so safe . . .": Coleman, *Lennon*, 507.

"When I slagged off . . .": Coleman, *Lennon*, 504.

"Why haven't I . . .": Coleman, *Lennon*, 506.

"It was lovely": Miles, *Paul McCartney*, 591.

"pretty chintzy" *Saturday Night Live*, November 20, 1976.

"I've always had . . .": Flippo, "The Private Years," in *The Ballad of John and Yoko*, 154.

"It's time to . . .": Cott, "The Last *Rolling Stone* Interview," in *The Ballad of John and Yoko*, 185.

"Here we are . . .": Sheff and Golson, *The Playboy Interviews*, 7.

"It's taken . . .": Cott, "The Last *Rolling Stone* Interview," in *The Ballad of John and Yoko*, 190.

"You breathe in . . .": Sheff and Golson, *The Playboy Interviews*, 39.

"John, you're an idealist . . .": Coleman, *Lennon*, 580.

"I'm shot . . .": Coleman, *Lennon*, 584.

"John would have . . .": Coleman, *Lennon*, 588.

"John loved . . .": Flippo, "Sharing the Grief," in *The Ballad of John and Yoko*, 207.

Afterword

"What's talent . . .": Giuliano, *Two of Us*, 27.

"mulling over past . . ." "Especially Strawberry . . ." and "For John . . .": Martin and Pearson, *With a Little Help From My Friends*, 24.

"We all cried so hard . . .": Miles, *Paul McCartney*, 595.

"As far as . . .": Elliott, *The Mourning of John Lennon*, 155.

"Oh! This could . . .": Du Noyer, "But Now They're Really Important," *Q Magazine*, Dec. 1995, 121.

"The last time . . .": Elliott, *The Mourning of John Lennon*, 162.

"The three of . . .": Du Noyer, "But Now They're Really Important," *Q Magazine*, Dec. 1995, 123.

"Sometimes I walk . . .": Giuliano, *Lennon in America*, 222.

"Motherhood is . . .": Seabrook, "At Tea: Cognito," *The New Yorker*, 35.

"The thing . . .": Wiener, *Come Together*, 305.

"I want people . . .": Wenner, *Lennon Remembers*, 89.

BIBLIOGRAPHY

Baird, Julia, with Geoffrey Giuliano. *John Lennon: My Brother*. New York: Henry Holt, 1988. Reprint, New York: Jove Books, 1989.

Best, Pete, and Patrick Doncaster. *Beatle! The Pete Best Story*. New York: Dell Publishing Co., 1985.

Brown, Peter, and Steven Gaines. *The Love You Make: An Insider's Story of the Beatles*. New York: McGraw-Hill Book Co., 1983.

Chaucer, Geoffrey. "The Nun's Priest's Tale" and "The Miller's Tale" from *The Canterbury Tales* translated by Nevill Coghill. London: Penguin Classics, 1951. Fourth revised edition, 1977.

Clayson, Alan. *George Harrison*. London: Sanctuary Publishing Ltd., 2001.

_____. *Woman: The Incredible Life of Yoko Ono*. New Malden, Surrey: Chrome Dreams Publication, 2004.

Coleman, Ray. *Lennon*. New York: McGraw-Hill, 1985.

Cott, Jonathan. "Yoko Ono and Her Sixteen Track Voice." In *The Ballad of John and Yoko*, edited by Jonathan Cott and Christine Doudna. A Rolling Stone Press Book. Garden City, N.Y.: Doubleday, 1982.

_____. "The Last *Rolling Stone* Interview." In *The Ballad of John and Yoko*, edited by Jonathan Cott and Christine Doudna. A Rolling Stone Press Book. Garden City, N.Y.: Doubleday, 1982.

Davies, Hunter. *The Beatles: The Classics, Newly Revised*. 2nd revised edition. New York: W. W. Norton and Co., 1996.

_____. *The Quarrymen*. London: Omnibus Press (a Division of Music Sales Limited), 2001.

Ehrlichman, John. *Witness to Power: The Nixon Years*. New York: Simon and Schuster, 1982.

Elliott, Anthony. *The Mourning of John Lennon*. Berkeley: University of California Press, 1999.

Flippo, Chet. "The Private Years." In *The Ballad of John and Yoko*, edited by Jonathan Cott and Christine Doudna. A Rolling Stone Press Book. Garden City, N.Y.: Doubleday, 1982.

_____. "Sharing the Grief." In *The Ballad of John and Yoko*, edited by Jonathan Cott and Christine Doudna. A Rolling Stone Press Book. Garden City, N.Y.: Doubleday, 1982.

BIBLIOGRAPHY

Friedman, Robert, and David Friend, editors. *The Beatles: From Yesterday to Today*. Second edition. New York: Time Inc. Home Entertainment, 2001.

Giuliano, Geoffrey. *Lennon in America: Based in Part on the Lost Lennon Diaries 1971–1980*. New York: Cooper Square Press, 2000.

_____. *The Lost Beatle Interviews*. New York: Dutton, 1994.

_____. *Two of Us: John Lennon and Paul McCartney Behind the Myth*. New York: Penguin Putnam, 1999.

Gleason, Ralph. "Fair Play for John and Yoko." In *The Ballad of John and Yoko*, edited by Jonathan Cott and Christine Doudna. A Rolling Stone Press Book. Garden City, N.Y.: Doubleday, 1982.

Goldberg, Danny. *Dispatches from the Culture Wars: How the Left Lost Teen Spirit*. New York: Miramax Books, 2003.

Halberstam, David. *The Fifties*. New York: Random House, Villard Books, 1993.

Hamill, Pete. "Long Day's Journey into Night." In *The Ballad of John and Yoko*, edited by Jonathan Cott and Christine Doudna. A Rolling Stone Press Book. Garden City, N.Y.: Doubleday, 1982.

Harry, Bill. *The John Lennon Encyclopedia*. London: Virgin Publishing Ltd., 2000.

Henke, James. *Lennon Legend: An Illustrated Life of John Lennon*. San Francisco: Chronicle Books, 2003.

Hertsgaard, Mark. *A Day in the Life: The Music and Artistry of the Beatles*. New York: Dell Publishing, 1995.

Jerry, Hopkins. *Yoko Ono*. New York: Macmillan Publishing Co., 1986.

Kemp, Mark. "She Who Laughs Last: Yoko Ono Reconsidered." *Music Alternatives* (July–August 1992).

Kirk, Donald. "In Tokyo." In *The Ballad of John and Yoko*, edited by Jonathan Cott and Christine Doudna. A Rolling Stone Press Book. Garden City, N.Y.: Doubleday, 1982.

Kurlansky, Mark. *1968: The Year That Rocked the World*. New York: Ballantine Books, 2003.

Lennon, Cynthia. *A Twist of Lennon*. London: W.H. Allen & Co. Ltd, 1978.

Lennon, John. "Have We All Forgotten What Vibes Are?" In *The Ballad of John and Yoko*, edited by Jonathan Cott and Christine Doudna. A Rolling Stone Press Book. Garden City, N.Y.: Doubleday, 1982.

_____. *Skywriting by Word of Mouth and Other Writings, Including the Ballad of John and Yoko*. New York: Harper and Row, Publishers, 1986; reprint, New York: Perennial Library Edition, 1987.

Lewisohn, Mark. *The Complete Beatles Chronicle*. London: Pyramid Books, an imprint of Octopus Illustrated Publishing, 1992.

Marcus, Greil. "The Beatles." In *The* Rolling Stone *Illustrated History of Rock and Roll*. ed. Anthony De Curtis and James Henke with Holly George-Warren. New York: Random House, 1980.

Martin, George, with Jeremy Hornsby. *All You Need Is Ears*. New York: St. Martin's Press, 1979.

Martin, George, and William Pearson. *With a Little Help from My Friends: The Making of Sgt. Pepper*. Boston, Little Brown and Co., 1995.

Miles, Barry. *Paul McCartney: Many Years from Now*. New York: Henry Holt and Co., 1997.

_____, compiler. *John Lennon in His Own Words*. London: Omnibus Press, 1980; reprint, 1994.

Munro, Alexandra, with Jon Hendricks. *Yes Yoko Ono*. New York: Harry Abrams, Inc. 2000.

Norman, Philip. *Shout!: The Beatles in Their Generation*. New York: Simon and Schuster, 1981. Revised updated edition, 2003.

Ono, Yoko. *Grapefruit: A Book of Instructions and Drawings*. New York: Simon & Schuster, 1970. Reissue, 2000.

_____. "My Love, My Struggle." *Bungei Shunju* magazine, volume 52, no. 10-12, 1974. Translation provided by Kyoko K. Bischof.

Pang, May, and Henry Edwards. *Loving John: The Untold Story.* Book club edition. New York: Warner Books Inc., 1983.

Seabrook, John. "At Tea: Cognito." *The New Yorker*, May 19, 2003.

Sheff, David. "Playboy Interview: John Lennon and Yoko Ono." *Playboy* magazine, January 1981.

_____, and G. Barry Golson. *The Playboy Interviews with John Lennon and Yoko Ono*. New York: Playboy Press, a division of PEI Books Inc., 1981.

Shotton, Pete, and Nicholas Schaffner. *John Lennon in My Life*. Briarcliff Manor, N.Y.: Stein and Day, 1983.

Siegel, Joel. "Back in the U.S.S.A." In *The Ballad of John and Yoko*, edited by Jonathan Cott and Christine Doudna. A Rolling Stone Press Book. Garden City, N.Y.: Doubleday, 1982.

Solt, Andrew, and Sam Egan. *Imagine: John Lennon*. New York: Macmillan Co., 1988.

Sutcliffe, Pauline, with Douglas Thompson. *The Beatles' Shadow: Stuart Sutcliffe and His Lonely Hearts Club*. London: Sidgwick and Jackson, 2001. Reprint, London: Pan Books: 2002.

Taylor, Derek. *It Was Twenty Years Ago Today: An Anniversary Celebration of 1967*. New York: A Fireside Book published by Simon and Schuster, Inc., 1987.

Werbin, Stuart. "Some Time in New York City." In *The Ballad of John and Yoko*, edited by Jonathan Cott and Christine Doudna. A Rolling Stone Press Book. Garden City, N.Y.: Doubleday, 1982.

BIBLIOGRAPHY

Wenner, Jann S. "Lennon Remembers." In *The Ballad of John and Yoko*, edited by Jonathan Cott and Christine Doudna. A Rolling Stone Press Book. Garden City, N.Y.: Doubleday, 1982.

_____. *Lennon Remembers: The Full* Rolling Stone *Interviews from 1970*. New York: Straight Arrow Books, 1971. Reprint, New York: Verso, an Imprint of New Left Books, 2000.

White, Theodore H. *Breach of Faith: The Fall of Richard Nixon*. New York: Atheneum Publishers/Reader's Digest Press, 1975.

Wiener, Jon. *Come Together: John Lennon in His Time*. New York: Random House, 1984. Reissue, London: Faber and Faber, 1995.

_____. *Gimme Some Truth: The John Lennon FBI Files*. Berkeley: University of California Press, 1999.

Yorke, Ritchie. "Boosting Peace: John and Yoko in Canada." In *The Ballad of John and Yoko*, edited by Jonathan Cott and Christine Doudna. A Rolling Stone Press Book. Garden City, N.Y.: Doubleday, 1982.

FURTHER READING LIST

Biographies of John Lennon

Lennon: The Definitive Biography by Ray Coleman

Childhood

John Lennon: My Brother by Julia Baird with Geoffrey Giuliano

John Lennon in My Life by Pete Shotton and Nicholas Schaffner

Beatles Years

A Twist of Lennon by Cynthia Lennon

Post-Beatles Years

Loving John: The Untold Story by May Pang and Henry Edwards

Come Together: John Lennon in His Time by Jon Weiner

In-Depth, First-Person Interviews

The Playboy Interviews with John Lennon and Yoko Ono by David Sheff and G. Barry Golson

Lennon Remembers: The Full Rolling Stone *Interviews from 1970* by Jann S. Wenner

Beatles Books

The Beatles Anthology by The Beatles

The Beatles: The Classic, Newly Revised by Hunter Davies

The Complete Beatles Chronicle by Mark Lewisohn

Shout! The Beatles in Their Generation by Philip Norman

Primarily Photo Books

Lennon Legend: An Illustrated Life of John Lennon by James Henke

The Beatles: Ten Years That Shook the World by Paul Trynka

Imagine: John Lennon by Andrew Solt and Sam Egan

The Beatles: From Yesterday to Today by Robert Friedman and David Friend, editors

Books by Individual Photographers

Once There Was a Way . . . Photographs of the Beatles, by Harry Benson

Listen to These Pictures: Photographs of John Lennon by Bob Gruen

With the Beatles: The Historic Photographs of Dezo Hoffman, edited by Pearce Marchbank

Remember: The Recollections and Photographs of the Beatles by Michael McCartney

INDEX

Page numbers in **boldface** refer to captions of illustrations.

INDEX

ACKNOWLEDGMENTS

AS I IMMERSED myself in writing this biography, I was astonished both by John Lennon's brilliance and tender vulnerability and by how often he drove himself right to the edge. I feel a deep gratitude to the people who held him together when he needed it: Mimi Stanley Smith, Cynthia Lennon, Paul McCartney, and Yoko Ono Lennon.

My heartfelt thanks to Jill Davis, my perceptive editor, who threw herself into the project and shepherded it through many stages with great patience, wit, and humor. She further shone by being instrumental in locating and assembling the photographs. Our partnership was enhanced by the bold design work of Jim Hoover, who met our constant challenges with unbelievable creativity and grace. Janet Pascal went far beyond the usual role of copyeditor to smooth out rough patches, and even solicited needed musical advice from her brother, David Pascal. Further support at Viking was provided by Kati Banyai, Denise Cronin, Alex Gigante, Anne Gunton, Karen Mayer, Nico Medina, Rachel Nugent, John Vasile, and Doug Whiteman. Thanks to Lucy Del Priore, Lara Phan, and Keith Mutzman at Penguin. Special thanks to Regina Hayes for her vision, to Gerard Mancini for his complex and sensitive understanding of John and the Beatles' legacy, and to Aaron Whiteman for his kitchen-table wisdom. My agent, Ruth Cohen, was sterling.

My gratitude to Mark Naboshek, who provided memorabilia from his extensive Beatles collection, as well as John's school photographs, and introductions to several of John's Liverpool friends. Showing his Beatles scholarship and acumen, Mark was also the most enthusiastic and careful of fact-checkers.

For their vastly different perspectives on the sixties I thank Malcolm Margolin (unrepentant hippie) and Neil Smelser (scholar and college administrator). For his eloquence and inspiring love of gospel and rock'n'roll, John Delzel. For enriching my understanding of rock'n'roll as well as John Lennon, my thanks to James Henke, chief curator and head of exhibitions at the Rock and Roll Hall of Fame and Museum in Cleveland, Ohio. Jon Weiner was generous in helping me clarify details of John's immigration battle and place it in its important historical context.

Like many researchers, I take an intense pleasure in finding a photo that has never or rarely been published, or hearing the firsthand account of an incident that has become mythologized or lost in layers of speculation. Many people helped me as I tried to weave together interviews and photos to create a full picture of John's life. I began with what I skeptically assumed was one of the Lennon myths: that he was born the night of a bombing. Lorraine Chesters at National Museums Liverpool tracked down archival negatives of 1940 photographs taken the night before and the night of John's birth, showing the damage done by German bombers in Liverpool. John's childhood friend, Michael Hill, provided the photo of his school trip to Amsterdam, and his memories; Stanley Parkes, John's older cousin from Scotland, shared family photographs and a taste of the Stanley worldview that I had thought was uniquely John's, but which appears to ricochet throughout the family. Julia Baird, John's half-sister, made their mother's unique and spirited personality real for me.

John spoke frequently with reporters and authors, and I was able to weave together many of his firsthand accounts of his life. I am particularly grateful to Ray Coleman, Hunter Davies, David Sheff, and Jann Wenner. Cynthia Lennon, George Martin, May Pang, and Pete Shotton wrote fascinating books on their experiences with John (Martin also wrote about the other Beatles), and Barry Miles's biography of Paul McCartney was indispensable. For their scholarly books I am indebted to Mark Hertsgaard, Mark Lewisohn, and Jon Weiner.

Clearing permissions from multiple sources is a complex task, and Lourdes Lopez was incredibly diligent, clear-minded, and persistent in tracking down rights-holders. John's famous *Playboy* interviews were published separately in book and magazine form, and without the patient assistance of David Schmit at Playboy, I could not have attributed the quotes correctly. Kyoko K. Bischof's thoughtful translation for me of Yoko's revealing and vulnerable article "My Love, My Struggle," in *Bungei Shunju* magazine was crucial in my understanding of Yoko.

Thanks to the photographs taken and collected by a number of people, I was able to begin my book with John as a young child, and end with Annie Leibovitz's photograph taken just hours before John was killed. A number of photographers were generous and gracious with me: Frank Da Cruz, David Hurn, Tom Hanley, Cor Jaring, Astrid Kirchherr, Annie Leibovitz, Ken Light, Geoff Rhind, Charles Roberts, Ethan Russell, John Bigelow Taylor, Bob Whitaker, and Jurgen Vollmer. Additionally, many family members helped: Cor Jaring's son, Jeroen Jaring; Peter Moore's widow, Barbara Moore; John's cousin Stanley Parkes; Charles Robert's son Steve Roberts; and Charles Trainor's son, Charles Trainor, Jr.

A number of photo rights-holders, collectors, and archivists were indispensable. My admiration and gratitude to Kevin O'Sullivan at AP/Wideworld, Jeffrey Smith at Contact Press Images, Rod Davis of the Quarry Men, Anna Donohoe and Michelle Franklin at Getty Images, Michael Shulman at Magnum, Jonathan Hyams and Helen Ashford at Michael Ochs, Lisa Rayman at Mirrorpix, Mark Naboshek, Cecilia de Querol at Pacific Press Service, Christy Havranek at Retna, Valerie Bassett at Retrofile, Colleen Piano at Rex USA, and Ken Podsada and his knowledgeable staff, Bill May and Richard Kolnsberg, at Starfile. Chazz Avery and his Web site www.Beatlesource.com were brilliant.

Many thanks to Susan Campbell Bartoletti and my sister, Meg Partridge, who helped the manuscript immeasurably, as well as to big-hearted friends and family who stood on the sides of the racetrack shouting encouragement: Judy Blundell, Clair Brown, Julie Downing, Warren Franklin, Jeanine Gendar, Brian Hinch, Anna Grossnickle Hines and Gary Hines, Karen Kashkin, Stuart and Carrie Kutchins, Andrea Nachtigall, Rondal and Elizabeth W. Partridge, Cheryl Rhodes, Lucy Rush, and Katherine Tillotson.

My gratitude to my husband, Tom Ratcliff, who lived graciously and cheerfully with the specter of John Lennon for three years, and to my children, Will and Felix Ratcliff.

And special thanks to Sydney Feeney for her steady and fearless encouragement.

PERMISSIONS

I am grateful for permission to quote from the following sources:

"Yoko Ono and Her Sixteen Track Voice" by Jonathan Cott, "The Private Years" by Chet Flippo, "Fair Play for John and Yoko" by Ralph Gleason, "In Tokyo" by Donald Kirk, "Lennon Remembers" by Jann S. Wenner, and "Some Time in New York City" by Stuart Werbin, from *The Ballad of John and Yoko*. (A Rolling Stone Press Book. Garden City, N.Y.: Doubleday, 1982.) Copyright © Rolling Stone Press, 1982. Reprinted by permission of Rolling Stone LLC.

The Beatles: The Classics, Newly Revised by Hunter Davies. 2nd revised edition. Copyright © 1996, 1985, 1978, 1968 by Hunter Davies. Used by permission of W. W. Norton & Company, Inc.

"The Miller's Tale" from *The Canterbury Tales* by Geoffrey Chaucer, translated by Nevill Coghill (London: Penguin Classics, 1951; fourth revised edition, 1977). Copyright 1951 by Nevill Coghill. Copyright © the Estate of Nevill Coghill, 1958, 1960, 1975, 1977. Reproduced by permission of Penguin Books, Ltd.

Come Together: John Lennon and His Time by Jon Wiener (New York: Random House, 1984). Reissue (London: Faber and Faber, 1995). Copyright © 1984, 1985, by John Wiener, Introduction © 1993 by John Wiener. Reprinted with the kind permission of the author.

The Complete Beatles Chronicle by Mark Lewisohn (London: Pyramid Books, an imprint of Octopus Illustrated Publishing, 1992). Text copyright © 1992 by Mark Lewisohn. Reprinted with the kind permission of the author.

A Day in the Life: The Music and Artistry of the Beatles by Mark Hertsgaard (New York: Dell Publishing, 1995). Copyright © 1995 by Mark Hertsgaard. Reprinted by permission of The Ellen Levine Agency, Trident Media.

The Fifties by David Halberstam. Copyright © 1993 by The Amateurs Limited. Used by permission of Villard Books, a division of Random House, Inc.

Imagine: John Lennon by Andrew Solt and Sam Egan. Copyright © 1988 by Andrew Solt and Sam Egan. Reprinted with the permission of Sarah Lazin Books.

The John Lennon Encyclopedia by Bill Harry. Copyright © Bill Harry, 2000. Used by permission of Virgin Publishing Ltd.

PHOTOGRAPH CREDITS